Men-at-Arms • 421

The Sikh Army 1799–1849

Ian Heath · Illustrated by Michael Perry

First published in Great Britain in 2005 by Osprey Publishing,
Midland House, West Way, Botley, Oxford OX2 0PH, UK
44-02 23rd St, Suite 219, Long Island City, NY 11101, USA
Email: info@ospreypublishing.com

Transferred to digital print on demand 2010

First published 2005
2nd impression 2009

Printed and bound by PrintOnDemand-Worldwide.com, Peterborough, UK

A CIP catalogue record for this book is available from the British Library

ISBN: 978 1 84176 777 2

Series Editor: Martin Windrow
Design by Alan Hamp
Index by Alan Thatcher
Originated by Grasmere Digital Imaging Ltd., Leeds, UK
Typeset in Helvetica Neue and ITC New Baskerville

Acknowledgements
The author would like to express his gratitude to Michael Perry, Norman Swales, Ian Knight and Tony Paul for their generosity
in providing illustrations for this book; additional thanks go to Michael not only for his usual exceptional attention to detail in
the preparation of the colour plates, but also for being such an all-round good egg.

Artist's note
Readers may care to note that the original paintings from which the colour plates in this book were prepared are available for
private sale. All reproduction copyright whatsoever is retained by the Publishers. All enquiries should be addressed to:

Michael Perry,
26 Fishpond Drive
The Park
Nottingham
NG7 1DG
UK

The Publishers regret that they can enter into no correspondence upon this matter.

The Woodland Trust
Osprey Publishing is supporting the Woodland Trust, the UK's leading woodland conservation charity, by funding the
dedication of trees.

www.ospreypublishing.com

THE SIKH ARMY 1799–1849

HISTORICAL BACKGROUND

FOLLOWING THE DEATH IN 1707 of the Mughal Emperor Aurangzeb, rivalry between the Mughals, Afghans and Persians had created a power vacuum in the Punjab, which left much of the province in the hands of a Sikh confederacy known as the *Khalsa* ('The Pure'). In 1748 the chiefs of this confederacy reorganized themselves into the *Dal Khalsa* or 'Army of the Pure', subdivided into 12 individual commands or *misls* ('equals') each under its own *misldar* or *sardar* (chief). These forces drove out the Mughals, repelled nine determined Afghan invasions, and in 1764 captured Lahore, traditional capital of the Punjab.

By the 1760s the *Dal Khalsa* had become the dominant power in the Punjab. Victory, however, had not led to peace, since the seizure of Mughal estates and property had resulted in territorial disputes between the *misls*, which took to fighting amongst themselves. Despite twice-yearly general assemblies of the entire *Dal Khalsa* at Amritsar, the absence of an overall leader meant that relations between the *misls* steadily worsened, and the unity of the *Khalsa* was compromised.

This was the situation when one Ranjit Singh, at the age of just 18 years, succeeded to the leadership of the Sukarchakia, by this time the paramount *misl*. After seizing Lahore from its ruling *misldar* by means of a ruse in July 1799, he embarked on a series of campaigns which forcibly reunited the *misls*, reduced many neighbouring states to tributary status, and led in time to the consolidation of the Punjab's patchwork of Sikh, Hindu and Muslim territories into a single unified state. This was the *Sarkar Khalsaji* ('the *Khalsa* State'), referred to by the British as the Kingdom of Lahore. The traditional Sikh system of government by assembly subsequently fell into abeyance; and in April 1801 Ranjit Singh proclaimed himself *Sarkar-i-wala*, or head of state – a title rendered by the British as Raja or, more often, Maharaja of Lahore.

Although in 1805 Ranjit was in fact just 'one of many chiefs' in the Punjab, continuous campaigning throughout his 40-year reign resulted in the steady expansion of his 'kingdom', as the remaining independent *misls* were subdued and territories initially obliged to pay tribute were

Muslim irregulars in the service of a senior *jagirdar* or feudal chief, painted by Emily Eden in December 1838. (ENI Library)

3

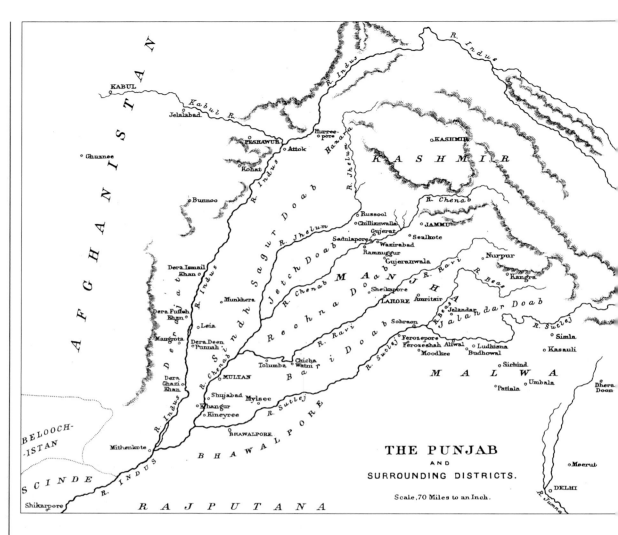

THE PUNJAB
AND
SURROUNDING DISTRICTS.

Scale, 70 Miles to an Inch.

The Punjab or 'Land of the Five Rivers' in the mid-19th century, from Gough's *The Sikhs and the Sikh Wars*. The five rivers were the Jhelum, Chenab, Ravi, Beas, and Sutlej. The principal engagements of both the First and Second Sikh Wars took place in the vicinity of the Sutlej.

progressively annexed. The extensive Multan district, under Afghan suzerainty but effectively an independent state, became part of Ranjit's dominions in 1818; and the conquest of Kashmir and Punchh in 1819 eliminated the last remaining vestiges of Afghan power east of the Indus.

Afghan ascendancy continued to wane as Ranjit's power waxed. The strategically important Peshawar valley west of the Indus was conquered following a Sikh victory over the Afghans at Naushehra in March 1823. However, at that date Ranjit did not consider his resources sufficient to annex the region outright, and he settled for a nominal payment of tribute. As a result Sikh and Afghan forces found themselves competing for control of Peshawar for many years thereafter, before it was finally annexed by Ranjit in May 1834.

There were two final Afghan attempts to recover Peshawar: in 1835, when the Afghan ruler Dost Mohammed Khan withdrew rather than risk battle; and in 1837, when his son Mohammed Akbar Khan was obliged to retire despite a pyrrhic victory over the Sikhs at Jamrud. During this same period the subordinate chiefs of Bannu, Dera Ghazi Khan, Dera Ismail Khan and Kohat, were also replaced by administrators appointed from Lahore.

4

Though Ranjit continued to harbour designs on Sind, Ghazni, and the independent cis-Sutlej Sikh states, all such ambitions were frustrated by treaties with the British, and Peshawar was the last significant addition to the kingdom in his lifetime. At his death in June 1839 the frontiers of the Sikh state extended from Peshawar in the north-west to the River Sutlej in the south-east, and from the Himalayas in the north-east to the confluence of the Indus and Chenab rivers in the south-west. Its population of perhaps three million – of whom only about one-sixth were Sikhs – had roughly doubled since 1799.

THE BIRTH OF THE SIKH ARMY

The *misl* chiefs had begun to create their own standing armies in the second half of the 18th century. Although there were a few infantry and a small amount of artillery (described in 1783 as 'so awkwardly managed and so ill attended to, that little benefit is derived from it'), these consisted predominantly of cavalry. All respectable Sikhs fought mounted, and an infantryman was held in universal contempt, being (in Lepel Griffin's words) 'left behind to garrison forts, to look after the women or to follow, as best he could, the fighting force, until he in turn could afford to change his status and buy or steal a horse for his own use'.

There are several estimates of the military potential of the *misls* at about the end of the 18th century, which suggest an overall strength of some 60–75,000 horse, up to 25,000 infantry, and 40 guns. Ranjit Singh's Sukarchakia *misl* was reputedly capable of fielding 22,000 horse and foot at about the time of his father Mahan Singh's death in 1792.

While appreciating the flexibility and manoeuvrability of traditional Sikh organization and tactics, Ranjit Singh was quick to recognize the advantages – at least over undisciplined native forces – enjoyed by armies which had adopted French or British military systems, and he determined to organize an army of his own along similar lines. This required a major change in Sikh thinking as regards the relative importance of the three arms of service. Cavalry would no longer be considered the dominant arm on a battlefield; instead, artillery and large masses of disciplined infantry would come to predominate.

The exact date of Ranjit's tactical epiphany is uncertain. Most probably his thinking was already heading in this direction at the beginning of his reign, possibly as a result of the success of the Irish adventurer George Thomas with disciplined sepoys in his invasions of Jind and Haryana in 1798–1800; or perhaps in consequence of seeing the French General Perron's forces in the service of Daulat Rao Sindhia in 1800. It may also have been prompted by an early realization that, at some point, he would probably have to confront the British.

Ranjit himself considered 1805 as the date of his final conversion, following Jaswant Rao Holkar's arrival in the Punjab accompanied by several disciplined battalions, and the evidence of his own eyes during a clandestine visit to the camp of the British army under Lord Lake which was pursuing Holkar. However, he seems already to have employed some Purbia (Hindustani) and Muslim ex-sepoys as early as 1802, following the disbandment of George Thomas' army, and more were recruited from Perron's dispersed forces in 1803

Dating to 1814, this horseman is typical of the *misldar* era and the early years of Ranjit Singh's reign. Bows had been largely abandoned in the second half of the 18th century, but continued to be carried by some irregular cavalrymen and *Akalis* until the 1840s. Most were of composite construction, but some were steel. (By permission of the British Library. Or.1248)

following their defeat by Lake. In addition Ranjit began to encourage sepoys employed by the East India Company (EIC) to desert to his service.

Though Sayyad Mohammed Latif, writing in the 1830s, describes Sikh regular infantry campaigning in Jhang in 1803, it is now generally believed that Ranjit's first disciplined battalion was raised in 1805. By 1807 at the latest he had raised three battalions of regular infantry, trained by a *naik* (corporal) who had deserted from the EIC. By 1808 some 1,500 men were organized into five battalions, and by 1811 more than 2,800 were organized into nine battalions. By 1813 these disciplined troops, commanded until his death in 1826 by *Diwan* Ganga Ram, were already competent enough to secure a decisive victory over the Afghans at the battle of Chuch.

Ranjit was nevertheless unable and unwilling to abandon the traditional Sikh military system entirely – not only because the majority of his *sardars* demonstrated a strong aversion to both discipline and the adoption of European methods, but also because it would take time to build his new disciplined force up to effective strength. By respecting the *sardars'* prejudices, he could continue to depend on their loyalty and their sizeable military resources. He nevertheless recognized the need to bring such irregular elements under more centralized control.

Maintaining the old irregular army alongside the new regular troops entailed dividing the kingdom's armed forces into two separate branches: the state army, and the *Jagirdari Fauj* or feudal army. The former comprised the new European-style regular units, known as the *Fauj-i-ain*, plus a central corps of irregular troops maintained by the state, consisting of the *Ghorchurras* or *Fauj-i-sowari* (irregular cavalry) and the *Fauj-i-qilajat* (fortress garrisons and guards).

THE REGULAR ARMY – *FAUJ-I-AIN*

The *Fauj-i-ain* or 'regular army' was also known as the *Fauj-i-qawa'idan* or 'drilled force', in order to distinguish it from those elements of the state army still organized along traditional lines – the *Ghorchurras* and the *Fauj-i-qilajat* – which were referred to instead as the *Fauj-i-beqawa'id* ('the force without drill') or *Fauj-i-ghair-ain* ('the force without regulations'). Being entirely Ranjit Singh's creation, the *Fauj-i-ain* was also sometimes referred to as the *Campu-i-mu'alla* (literally 'the exalted camp', meaning the Maharaja's own army). The *Fauj-i-ain* soon became the most effective branch of the Sikh army, and eventually comprised infantry, artillery, and cavalry.

From the very beginning, *Fauj-i-ain* infantry battalions bore testimony to their foreign roots by being called *palatan* (singular *paltan*), a corruption of the French word *peloton* ('company'). The earliest *paltans* were small, their size probably being determined not only by the limited abilities of their early instructors (all of whom seem previously to have held ranks no higher than corporal, whether in Holkar's, Sindhia's or EIC employ), but also by the difficulty of obtaining willing recruits, since the Punjabis, despising infantry service, were unwilling to submit to European-style drill.

To foreign eyes these early units were distinctly unimpressive. The five seen by Charles Metcalfe in 1808 comprised just 200–400 men each, armed with swords and a mixture of European muskets and traditional matchlocks. Nor were the men uniformed, Metcalfe observing that their only distinguishing item of dress was a scarlet turban. These units were so small that they were not even subdivided into companies. It took another decade or so for battalions to grow to more impressive proportions, and even longer before they settled to anything approaching a consistent size.

During the period c.1810–20 they generally ranged between 200 and 800 men, most consisting of about 400–600 men divided into between eight and 11 companies. Battalion officers in 1818 comprised a *kumedan* (commandant), *adjutan* (adjutant), *mahzor* (major, the battalion quartermaster), *hakim* (surgeon), *naqib* (advocate), *munshi* (scribe, secretary or interpreter), and *mutassadi* (accountant, clerk or comptroller) – the last two being responsible for duties pertaining to the muster rolls and managing and distributing the unit's pay. Each company, divided into two sections, was commanded by a *subedar* (captain) or sometimes a *jamadar* (lieutenant), assisted by two *havildars* (sergeants), two *naiks* (corporals), and a *tamburchi* (drummer).

The *Fauj-i-ain* continued to grow, reflecting the expansion of the Sikh state itself. There were nine battalions in 1812, and 12 by 1814. According to a surviving Sikh diary there were 14 battalions by 1815 and 16 by 1821; but official sources record

Fauj-i-ain infantryman, irregular infantryman, and regular infantry officer, c.1845. Many Sikh soldiers carried shields slung on their backs. A participant in the battle of Ramnagar in November 1848 describes how, when attacked by British cavalry, some Sikh infantry 'turned their backs, protected by a shield from the stroke of the Dragoon sabre, and the moment that was given, turned round, hamstrung the horse, and shot the rider'. (ENI Library)

Jean-Baptiste Ventura's background is uncertain. Some describe him rising to the rank of colonel of infantry in Napoleon's army, and fighting in Russia in 1812 and at Waterloo in 1815; but others claim that he performed no more than limited military service, as a dragoon, in 1814–15. Ventura subsequently served in the Turkish or Egyptian army, then the Persian, before being employed by Ranjit Singh in 1822.

just 13 battalions totalling 7,750 men in 1819, and 14 battalions in 1821. By 1823 there were 17 battalions, totalling some 11,680 men.

European instructors were introduced by Ranjit Singh in the 1820s (see below), and these influenced the development of unit organization thereafter. By the end of the decade battalion strengths had increased to an average of some 700–900 men (though actual strengths varied between 600 and 1,100). In the 1830s most battalions averaged 600–800 men, but the largest to be found in the payrolls during 1832–39 had as many as 1,150. *Fauj-i-ain* unit strengths continued to fluctuate even during the kingdom's last few years, with battalions varying between about 350 and 1,200 men in the 1840s. Surviving payrolls indicate that most fell somewhere between 800 and 1,000, but British officers at the time of the First Sikh War (1845–46) believed that '600 men constituted the full effective strength of each battalion'.

During the 1820s battalions began to be referred to as 'regiments' by their European instructors, and some units were paired to form two-battalion regiments for administrative purposes. Under most circumstances, however, battalions continued to operate as individual units. One-battalion 'regiments' continued at first to be commanded by *kumedans*, while two-battalion regiments were commanded by colonels; but before long it became commonplace for colonels to be found in command of single-battalion regiments too – the *kumedan*, in units that retained one, then became the second-in-command. The other officers of a battalion's command element now comprised *adjutan*, *mahzor*, *munshi*, *mutassadi*, and *granthi*, the last being the battalion chaplain. Although there were some exceptions (such as the *Gurkha Paltan*), most battalions were named after their commanding officer.

Standardized unit organization was an innovation of the army's European instructors. By 1828 at the latest battalions were customarily divided into eight companies regardless of size. The companies nominally consisted of 100 men (plus officers), initially organized into two sections but later into four. Each company was commanded by a *subedar*, with two *jamadars*, a *sarjan* (sergeant-major), and a *phuriya* (from the French word *fourrier*, or quartermaster sergeant). Each section was commanded by a *havildar* and a *naik*. Theoretically each company also had a *tambur mahzor* (drum major), a bugler, a trumpeter, and two or more drummers. Eyewitnesses also mention the use of fifes, while some battalions had entire bands.

The appearance of the ranks of *sarjan* and *phuriya* since 1818 was doubtless a direct result of French influence, after the Napoleonic Wars. The simultaneous disappearance of the *hakim* and *naqib* since 1818 was possibly the consequence of a dearth of suitably qualified men. Along with the *adjutan*, the *sarjan* and *phuriya* appear to have acted principally as aides to the company commander.

In addition to its combatant strength each battalion had a non-combatant establishment made up of paid servants referred to as *amla*. Ideally these were supposed to comprise four *gharyalis* (time-keepers, responsible for striking the hours on a gong); four *jhanda bardars* (flag-bearers, one per two companies, responsible for looking after the battalion colours); nine *khalasis* (tent-pitchers); 16 *saqqas* (water-carriers, two per company); 16 *langris* (cooks, two per company); eight *beldars* (sappers); nine *sarbans* (camel-drivers, in charge of the battalion's baggage camels), and a *harkara* (messenger or runner). In addition, battalions in the field were accompanied by a train of artisans including blacksmiths, masons, tailors and the like.

Discipline was reputedly severe, 'the rattan [cane] being liberally administered for trifling offences'. In 1838 W.G.Osborne reported that senior officers beat junior officers, and junior officers beat the men. Minor infractions, however, were chiefly punished by fines, extra duty, demotion, or imprisonment; but more serious offences might be punished by dismissal from the service, branding, and the mutilation or removal of the offender's hands, ears and/or nose. There was, however, no death penalty.

Fauj-i-ain pay was higher than that of the EIC. It could be disbursed in a variety of ways, but monthly cash wages eventually became the norm. Having said that, wages were rarely actually paid out monthly – delays in payment were a characteristic feature of service in every branch of the Sikh army; wages could be anything between four months and two years in arrears, and between six and 12 months' delay was common. Surprisingly, during Ranjit Singh's reign this caused fewer problems than might have been expected, since, as Charles Masson explained, 'the troops are not paid with punctuality, but they are certain of receiving all arrears once during the year'. The situation deteriorated in the 1840s, however, when there were numerous desertions and mutinies resulting from overdue pay. Average infantry monthly pay rates during Ranjit's reign were:

Sepoy	Rupees 7–8½
Naik	Rs 10–12
Havildar	Rs 12–16
Jamadar	Rs 15–20
Subedar	Rs 20–35
Mahzor	Rs 25–50
Adjutan	Rs 30–55
Kumedan	Rs 60–125
Colonel	Rs 250–325
General	Rs 375–450

A cavalry *sowar* received Rs 20–26, and a *risaldar* Rs 35–50; and artillerymen received much the same pay as infantrymen.

* * *

Surviving records indicate that the *Fauj-i-ain's* infantry strength continued to increase throughout the 1830s, from 21 battalions in 1831 to 31 by 1838, totalling some 20,000 men at the former date and nearly 27,000 at the latter. Several other contemporary sources put their strength even higher. In 1835, for instance, the *Delhi Gazette* reported the existence of 34 battalions, with a further 12 in the process of formation. In that same year, W.L.M'Gregor saw official Sikh records which listed 35 'Aeen' infantry battalions. In 1836 another

Ranjit Singh (seated in the armchair at left) holding council, from Osborne's *The Court and Camp of Runjeet Singh*. Hira Singh is seated opposite him. The row of European officers standing at the right are said to be Claude-Auguste Court, Jean-François Allard, Jean-Baptiste Ventura, Paolo di Avitabile, an Englishman named Foulkes (Ventura's aide-de-camp), and Benoit Argoud. Osborne was in the Punjab in 1838, but since Argoud was only in Ranjit's service in 1836–37 this engraving must be based on an earlier native painting. (ENI Library)

visitor reported 40 battalions, each of 1,000 men; but in 1838 Lord Auckland grossly overestimated the Sikh regular infantry at 70 battalions. William Barr reckoned that there were 50,000 regular infantrymen in 1839, a total not actually achieved until the mid-1840s. Such exaggerated claims, along with the very real growth in Ranjit Singh's military might, reflected the increasing tensions that now existed between the Sikhs and their British neighbours.

Indeed, by the end of Ranjit's reign a parade of his regular infantry was an awesome spectacle for British diplomats and officers to behold. Contradicting the disparaging views expressed in their official writings, Lord Auckland's sister Emily Eden candidly records the real opinion of such visitors following a parade observed in December 1838. She wrote that they found the Sikhs 'quite as well disciplined, rather better dressed', and capable of repeating the same military movements 'and several others much more complicated' as the British-Indian troops present on this occasion. 'Nobody knows what to say about it', she adds, 'so they say nothing, except that they are sure the Sikhs would run away in a real fight. It is a sad blow to our vanities!'

The French connection
Although Ranjit Singh had hired foreign military advisors from the outset, there were at first few Westerners among them. The very first European he employed – a British deserter named Price – was hired in 1809, and a handful of others probably followed during the next ten years; but most of Ranjit's earliest foreign instructors were Indians and Anglo-Indians. This changed with the conclusion of the Napoleonic Wars in 1815, which created a surfeit of experienced soldiers ready to sell their services to foreign potentates. During the 1820s and 1830s a steadily increasing number of these found their way into Sikh service.

With the increasing possibility of a collision with the British foremost in his mind, Ranjit made a specific point of hiring Frenchmen and Italians when he could, especially those who had served under Napoleon. Indeed, British agents believed that the return of one such officer to France on leave in 1834 was accompanied by a specific request from Ranjit to King Louis-Philippe for additional French officers for his army. Nevertheless, British and Anglo-Indian officers and deserters continued to be taken on (they were, after all, ready to hand), and other nationalities were not neglected.

Though their exact number is unknown, there may have been 50 or so foreign officers by the end of Ranjit's reign, while some modern authorities mention figures as high as 100 and even 200. According to J.D.Cunningham there were 32 in about 1843, while G.C.Smyth and Alexander Gardner (himself one of them) mention 39 such men. Of these totals, Smyth says that 12 were French, seven Anglo-Indian, four British, four Italian, three American, three German, two Greek, two Spanish, one Prussian and one Russian; while Gardner says that there were 13 Frenchmen, seven 'Englishmen', six Anglo-Indians, four Italians, two Americans, two Greeks, two Spaniards, two Russians and one German. All but one of the so-called 'Americans' employed at one time or another were actually British deserters attempting to disguise their origins.

Many of the foreigners in Ranjit Singh's employ were unsavoury characters of dubious background, but others had led faultless military careers, especially the French and Italian officers (who are consequently described as having 'held much aloof from those of the other nationalities'). Foremost among these were four ex-Napoleonic officers: Jean-Francois Allard and Jean-Baptiste Ventura, hired in 1822, and Paolo di Avitabile and Claude Auguste Court, hired in 1827. Although Ranjit regarded most of his foreigners as little more than highly paid and not entirely trustworthy drill sergeants, these four at least had a significant impact on the development of his army, most notably in the improvement of his artillery and the creation of the elite *Fauj-i-khas*.

Needless to say, with their sometimes huge salaries (most received between Rs 300 and 800 per month, and Allard and Ventura were paid Rs 3,000) and their grants of estates and administrative posts (Ventura and Avitabile were appointed provincial governors), Ranjit's foreign officers were not popular amongst the Sikh *sardars*. As early as 1833 one English visitor observed that the *sardars'* feelings towards them were such 'as to make the situation of these officers very hazardous and delicate in the event of Runjeet Singh's decease'. Their personal safety was further compromised when, in the years of anarchy which followed Ranjit's death, elements of the army supported one or another claimant to the throne, and several foreign officers were murdered by their own troops.

Unsurprisingly, therefore, many foreigners left as the country's political instability worsened, most particularly after Maharaja Sher Singh's assassination in 1843 (Ventura, Court, and Avitabile all departed at this juncture; Allard had died in 1839). Sikh confidence in the remaining foreigners waned as the inevitability of war with the British increased. In June 1844, the child Maharaja Dalip Singh's advisors 'represented that the East Indian and French officers, employed in several situations with the Sikh troops, would desert when battle should take place with the English, and that therefore they had better be discharged at once.' The majority were accordingly dismissed, the most notable of the few exceptions being the Anglo-Indians John Holmes and Henry Charles van Cortlandt, and a Spanish engineer named Hurbons. A few others were subsequently re-enlisted, including a French cavalry officer named Francois Henry Mouton and an English artillerist, Richard Potter.

Only three foreign officers – Hurbons, Mouton, and Potter – are specifically known to have served in the field against the British during the Sikh Wars, but a handful of less significant individuals – the sort of

Drill instructions, from a Sikh *Zafarnama* (military manual) translated c.1822–30 from an infantry manual that either Allard or Ventura (probably the latter) had brought from France. The commands remain in French – the 'official language' of the *Fauj-i-khas* – although rendered in Persian script. The soldiers wear *Fauj-i-khas* uniforms of blue turban, red jacket with yellow facings, black cross belts and white trousers. (Tony Paul)

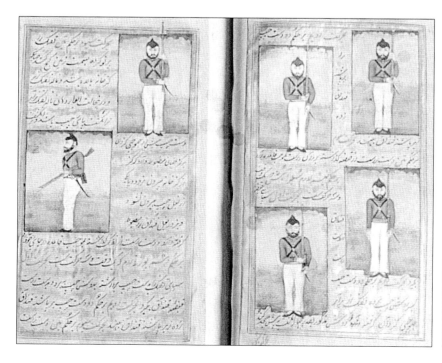

riffraff whom Henry Lawrence described in 1845 as 'deserters and vagabond Franks.. receiving ten shillings a day' - are recorded as being killed or captured by the British. These included a certain Barlow, ex-44th Foot, killed at Ferozeshah; and Boyle and Lairdie, two EIC deserters killed at the battle of Sobraon.

A clause of the Treaty of Lahore drawn up in 1846 after the First Sikh War ordained that henceforth no European or American could enter Sikh service without the permission of the British. Only a handful of foreign officers remained in the Punjab

Paintings of a Sikh regular drummer and a soldier in native dress. They appear on a leaf from one of many similar volumes of pictures by native artists - copied from earlier originals - produced to satisfy the British tourist trade in about 1860. The drummer wears white turban and trousers and a red jacket with yellow braiding and blue cuffs; he appears to have closed black shoes. The matchlock-man has a white turban, greyish-purple coat, yellow shawl/sash, white trousers, and slippers. (By permission of the British Library. Or.1423)

thereafter – John Holmes, killed by his own mutinous troops in October 1848, was the last of them.

The royal army – *Fauj-i-khas*

Though European-style discipline and training had been introduced in the Sikh army well before Allard's and Ventura's arrival in 1822, it was they who brought 'a moderate degree of precision and completeness' to the system. They were granted almost unlimited authority in organizing new units, and advised on the promotion and appointment of their officers. Ranjit ordered the commanders of his existing *Fauj-i-ain* battalions to adopt French drill and training methods in place of the British system previously followed, and any opposition by his *sardars* was punished. In reality, however, the change was gradual and never completed, since as late as 1838 at least two or three battalions continued to be trained along British lines.

Just two months after their arrival, Allard and Ventura created the elite *Fauj-i-khas* or 'royal army', an independent brigade that was to become known as the *Francese Campu* or 'French Legion'. Allard was simultaneously appointed commander of all *Fauj-i-ain* cavalry, including those of the Legion. The Legion's infantry element at first comprised just two battalions (the *Paltan Khas* and *Paltan Dewa Singh*), with a combined strength of some 1,200 men. In June 1823 a third battalion (the *Gurkha Paltan*) was added, increasing infantry strength to about 2,000. A fourth battalion (the *Paltan Sham Sota*) followed in 1824.

The Legion's cavalry element was organized from scratch; Allard raised two regiments, the *Rajman Khas Lansia* ('Royal Lancer Regiment') and the *Rajman Daragun Anwal* ('First Dragoon Regiment'). In addition the brigade had an attached artillery corps under the command of a Muslim officer, Ilahi Bakhsh. This is usually reported to have comprised 24 guns, but actually seems to have had about 15 to 20 serviceable pieces. Four infantry battalions and two cavalry regiments plus artillery remained the usual strength of the *Fauj-i-khas* thereafter, although for a brief period during 1826–27 Ranjit increased it to five infantry battalions and three cavalry regiments. It had three cavalry units again by 1845.

Visiting British officers all commented on the Legion's French drill. Osborne observed in June 1838 that its infantry 'work in three ranks, and do everything by beat of drum, according to the French fashion'. All words of command were given in French, and the Legion's French inspiration was further emphasized by its tricolour flags topped by Imperial eagles. These flags differed from their Napoleonic counterparts only in bearing inscriptions in Persian script, most often *'deg tegh fateh'* ('cauldron, sword, victory'), the motto of the *Khalsa*. Claude Court records that Ranjit Singh 'saw no harm' in Ventura's and Allard's adoption of such flags, 'knowing that we had all fought under the flag of Napoleon I'.

A measure of the effectiveness of the corps' French training may be seen in Osborne's comment that its troops could shoot 'with greater precision and regularity, both volleys and file firing, than any other troops I ever saw'. Following the Sikh Wars, veterans of the Peninsula and Waterloo campaigns opined that the Legion's fire was 'both better delivered and better aimed than that of the Napoleonic infantry'.

Needless to add, the *Fauj-i-khas* soon became the Sikh army's best drilled, best uniformed, best armed, and best equipped corps. It served at Naushehra (1823); in Dera Ismail Khan, Multan, and Peshawar (1837–39); in the conquest of Kulu and Mandi (1841); and during the First Sikh War (1845–46). Its strength had reached some 5,500 men by the end of the 1830s and was much the same at the outbreak of war with the British in 1845, when it comprised 3,176 infantry, 1,667 cavalry, and 855 artillerymen with 34 guns. By this time the *Paltan Khas* stood at 820 men, the *Gurkha Paltan* at 707, the *Paltan Dewa Singh* at 839, and the *Paltan Sham Sota* at 810. Its cavalry now comprised the 'Grenadier Regiment' (730 men), the First Dragoons (750 men), and 'a troop of life guards', presumably the Royal Lancers (187 men).

Because of Allard's other commitments, the Legion was effectively (and actually, after his death in 1839) under Ventura's command until his departure for France in 1843. He was then succeeded by his deputy, *Diwan* Ajudhia Prashad (nephew of *Diwan* Ganga Ram), who commanded the *Fauj-i-khas* during the First Sikh War.

Other brigades

The gradual organization of the *Fauj-i-ain* into brigades in the 1820s and 1830s was an obvious consequence of European influence. The French Legion or *Francese Campu*, established in 1822, had been the first; and this was followed in about 1827 by the *Campu Oms*, of five infantry battalions and one cavalry regiment under a Spaniard named Oms, who died in 1828. By 1830 Avitabile and Court also commanded brigades, each of three battalions and a handful of guns. Not until 1831 do we encounter such an all-arms corps being commanded by a Punjabi, when James Skinner records seeing a brigade led by one Nawab Amir Khan, of two or three infantry battalions, '2,000–3,000' cavalry (much more probably, 200–300), and 'some' artillery. A brigade structure was eventually adopted for the rest of the *Fauj-i-ain* in 1835.

Table 1: Fauj-i-ain strength, 1811–45 *(After Sita Ram Kohli)*

Date	Infantry	Cavalry	Artillery	Total
1811	2,852	1,209	–	14,061
1819	7,748	750	834	9,332
1823	11,681	1,656	1,688	15,025
1828	15,825	4,345	3,778	23,948
1833	20,577	3,914	8,162	32,653
1838	26,617	4,090	4,535	35,242
1843	37,791	5,381	8,280	51,452
1845	53,962	6,235	10,524	70,721

There were no hard and fast rules defining the preferred strength and constitution of a brigade. Most often, however, they consisted of three or four infantry battalions, a detachment of cavalry (usually anything from a company to a regiment), one or – less often – two batteries of artillery, a company of *beldars* (sappers), and its own commissariat. Some, however, lacked either guns or cavalry, while others included detachments of 'irregulars' (actually the drilled troops of leading *jagirdars* or feudal landowners – see below). The entire corps normally totalled some 4,000–5,000 men and 10–25 guns.

At their initial introduction in 1835 there were probably eight brigades (including the *Fauj-i-khas*), since most brigades were commanded by generals, and Ranjit Singh created eight generals when he introduced the rank in 1836. These were Ventura, Court, Ajit Singh, Gujar Singh, Ram Singh, Tej Singh, Misr Sukh Raj, and Mian Udham Singh (Allard was on leave in France). By 1845, however, there were 12 brigades (as well as numerous independent battalions and batteries), and the commanders of some were mere colonels.

In 1838 Ranjit had planned to create an 'English Brigade' along the same lines as, and presumably as a counterbalance to, the French Legion. This was to be commanded by Matthew Ford, sometime paymaster of the British 16th Foot (from which he had deserted in 1837) and subsequently a battalion commander in Avitabile's brigade. Ford was instructed 'to form a brigade to be called the English Brigade, and to be composed from his own battalion, that of Cortlandt, and another to be collected'. The plan never came to fruition, however, and Ford was killed by his own troops in 1841.

Until the mid-1840s there was no level of organization above that of brigade, and individual brigades were in effect independent commands. In 1844, however, it was proposed that four divisions should be created; and in November of the following year British intelligence reported the existence of seven divisions, each some 8,000–12,000 strong. Details are provided for the composition of only three of these. One consisted of 4,000 horse and two infantry brigades under Sham Singh Atariwala; another, of 4,500 horse and two infantry brigades under Raja Lal Singh; and the third, of 1,000 horse and four infantry brigades (including one of 'irregulars') under *Sardar* Tej Singh.

Army commanders were appointed on a temporary basis for the duration of each campaign, and were given as many battalions, brigades, or divisions as were deemed necessary for the task in hand. Nor was there at first an overall commander-in-chief; Ranjit Singh retained this post in his own hands until 1826, when it passed to the heir apparent, Kharak Singh, who held it until his death in 1840.

The regular cavalry

There were three types of cavalry in the *Khalsa* army: regulars, *Ghorchurras*, and *Jagirdari*.

The regular cavalry are first mentioned in 1819, when they are recorded as consisting of just 837 men organized in three *rajmans* (regiments). A fourth regiment was added in 1821. Real improvements in this arm only began with the appointment of Jean-Francois Allard as commander of the regular cavalry in 1822, since it was he who introduced European-style training and tactics (whence regular cavalrymen were known as 'French sowars', *sowaran Francees*). It was an uphill struggle, however, since Ranjit Singh was far more concerned with improving the quality of his infantry and artillery, and considered that his numerous *Ghorchurras* and *Jagirdari* horse precluded the need for a sizeable regular cavalry force. In addition, his subjects demonstrated a marked reluctance to enlist as regular cavalrymen, preferring to perform their mounted service in the traditional Sikh style.

Starved of funds, official interest and public enthusiasm, the regular cavalry remained decidedly second-rate even at the end of Ranjit's reign. In 1838, for instance, Osborne described a detachment as 'men of all ages, ill-looking, ill-dressed, and worse mounted... Neither in appearance nor in reality are they to be compared to the infantry soldier of the Panjab. One reason for this is that Ranjit personally inspects every recruit for his infantry, while the cavalry is generally recruited from the followers of the Sardars, and most of them owe their appointment to favour and interest more than to fitness and capability.'

As we have seen, the first two European-style regiments (the *Rajman Khas Lansia* and *Rajman Daragun Anwal*) were raised by Allard in 1822. Several more regiments were created during the next few years: a second dragoon regiment existed by 1823, and another lancer regiment by January 1827. Others included the *Rajman Sheikh Qamar ud-Din*, the *Rajman Gulab*, the *Rajman Akal*, and a unit referred to in British sources as the 'Grenadier Regiment'. All of these were apparently trained and equipped as dragoons, since a description of the *Khalsa*'s regular cavalry in 1838 describes it as consisting of two regiments of lancers and six of dragoons. (Writing in 1829, however, Masson considered all but the lancers and the two regiments specifically designated as dragoons to be equivalent to light cavalry.) In 1836, orders were issued for the raising of two regiments of cuirassiers, though this was apparently not achieved until 1839.

Irregularities in funding led to some regiments enjoying no more than a fleeting existence, and ensured that most remained constantly under strength. Regiments were demobilized and re-formed almost on a whim. There were four regiments in 1824, seven in 1828, eight in 1829, six in 1830, and five in 1831, while a visitor wrote in 1834 that 'of the regiments of cavalry raised by M.Allard, but one remains, the others having been dispersed'. There were nevertheless eight regiments again by 1838, ten in 1839, 12 in 1843, eight in 1844, 15 in 1845, and seven in 1847. Their individual strengths could vary equally dramatically, from a hundred men up to a thousand. The smallest on record was the *Rajman Gobind*, which in 1839 numbered just 98 men. However, most regiments fell somewhere in the range 200–500 men in the 1830s, and 250–700 in

This engraving in Honigberger's *Thirty-Five Years in the East* (1852), copied from a native painting that must have been collected some time between 1839 and 1849, appears to be the only known contemporary picture of a Sikh *charaina sowar* or cuirassier (see Plate F1). John Martin Honigberger was a Transylvanian doctor, employed by Ranjit Singh and his successors as superintendent of a gunpowder factory in Lahore. (ENI Library)

Sikh regular cavalryman of an unnamed regiment, 1838. His red-decorated lance, the lion on his saddlecloth, and his white trousers might suggest a sowar of the *Rajman Khas Lansia*, even though the colour of his jacket (red with dark blue facings) is wrong. Note his highly unusual tasselled red cap, clearly inspired by a French *bonnet de police*. The saddle cloth is of red bordered with dark blue, of the same shades as the uniform; the lion is in natural colours. (By permission of the British Library. Or.1384)

the 1840s. The British considered a typical Sikh cavalry regiment to comprise 600 men.

The regiments bore either versions of European names (the Dragoon, Grenadier, and Lancer regiments), religious names (the *Akal Ram*, and *Gobind* regiments), or were named after their commanding officers. The large regiments were divided into varying numbers of *risalas* or troops depending on their strength. Regimental staff comprised a colonel or *kumedan* (or both), *adjutan*, *mahzor*, *mutassadi*, *munshi*, *granthi*, and trumpet major. Each *risala* consisted of a *risaldar* (captain), two *jamadars*, a *nishanchi* (ensign), a *sarjan*, four *havildars*, four *naiks*, two trumpeters, and most often somewhere between 150 and 200 men. The regiment's non-combatant establishment theoretically comprised four time keepers, four flag-bearers, nine tent-pitchers, five blacksmiths, four carpenters, eight sappers, and nine water-carriers.

Whatever level of efficiency the regular cavalry achieved (most British observers considered this to be minimal) largely disappeared following Allard's death in 1839. Certainly the regular regiments were thereafter considered sufficiently irrelevant by the British that by the outbreak of the First Sikh War in 1845 some believed that the whole arm had been abolished. This was not, of course, the case, and the regular cavalry actually reached its greatest ever strength in 1845; but when it came to war with the British, the Sikh regular cavalry invariably found itself unable to resist 'the impetuous charge of European dragoons'.

THE CAVALRY ARMY – GHORCHURRA FAUJ

The *Fauj-i-sowari* or 'cavalry army' was more popularly known as the *Ghorchurra Fauj*. The term *Ghorchurra* meant simply 'horseman', and was widely employed in the Punjab to describe irregular cavalry in general. In *Khalsa* administrative terms, however, it specifically denoted those irregular horsemen who received pay from the state, as distinct from those maintained by the feudal *sardars*. In reality the two types differed but little in either organization or lack of discipline.

The *Ghorchurras* of the *Fauj-i-sowari* were subdivided into the *Ghorchurra Khas* (Royal *Ghorchurras*) and the *Misldar Sowaran*. The former constituted a single regiment that eventually numbered some 1,600–2,000 men, made up predominantly of distinguished *sardars* and their kinsmen, and was the very first unit of standing troops that Ranjit Singh created. It was subsequently joined by a second regiment called the *Ardaly Khas* (Royal Orderlies), which appears to have been of similar composition and size. The *Ghorchurra Khas* and *Ardaly Khas* are frequently described as 'the Maharaja's bodyguard' by foreign visitors, who were much impressed by their colourful appearance and high spirits, and considered them 'the elite of the army', superior even to the French Legion.

The *Misldar Sowaran* consisted instead of troops taken into the Maharaja's service following either the death of their feudal overlord, the conquest of a neighbouring province, or the defeat of a rival *misldar* as the Sikh state expanded. Unsurprisingly, their numbers steadily increased throughout the existence of the Sikh kingdom, and they soon formed the greater part of the *Fauj-i-sowari*.

Overall, *Ghorchurra* strength stood at just 374 men in 1813, but had increased to 2,464 by 1817; to 7,300 by 1823; to 10,795 by 1838; and to 14,383 by 1843. A British estimate put them at 30,000 men in January 1845, but surviving Sikh records indicate that there were probably no more than 22,000.

The fact that the *Ghorchurras* were paid by the state led some visitors to consider them 'regular' troops, even though they never underwent any form of training or discipline. Their pay initially took the form of grants of land called *jagirs*, but by 1813 some had begun to be paid in coin; Ranjit Singh's ambition was to substitute cash wages for all their *jagirs* and thereby to put the entire *Ghorchurra* force on a more regular footing. The *Ghorchurras* nevertheless objected at first to receiving their pay in cash, considering that this demeaned them to the status of mercenaries.

About 5,000 *Ghorchurras* were being paid in cash by 1821, but it took several more years for the majority to be converted to the new system. By 1840, 10,559 were paid in cash and only 1,210 in *jagirs*, while by 1845 these figures stood at 19,626 and 1,613 respectively. The *jagirs* were customarily worth about Rs 400–600 per annum, while the cash wages started at around Rs 250–300. Most *Ghorchurra* cavalrymen received higher pay than their *Fauj-i-ain* counterparts, but had to provide their own arms, horses, and provisions. Missing items of equipment were provided by the state or by the *sardar* in whose company they served, but the cost was recovered from their pay by instalments.

Ghorchurra organization was into units called *derahs* ('camps'), which were mostly named after their original leader or, sometimes, their place of origin. Differing in size from a mere 150 men up to as many as 2,800, these units were subdivided into squadrons of equally varied strength, still known by the old name of *misls*. Each *misl* usually consisted of members of a single clan under its own chief, who was usually referred to as its *risaldar*. The smallest *misls* comprised no more than half-a-dozen closely related kinsmen, but the majority had somewhere between 15 and 75 troopers. From 1835 onwards some *derahs* had units of camel-mounted swivel guns attached to them.

The *derah* commander was a *sardar* holding no particular rank, his status and pay being entirely

Ghorchurra cavalrymen of Ranjit Singh's *Ghorchurra Khas* or *Ardaly Khas* regiments, from a British-commissioned Sikh painting captioned 'Lahore Life Guards 1838'. See Plate H1. (By permission of the British Library. Or.1385)

Ghorchurras collide with a squadron of the 3rd Light Dragoons at the battle of Chillianwalla, 13 January 1849. The British discovered in such encounters that Sikh cavalrymen were much better equipped than they for close combat, having sharper and better-made swords and effective protection in the form of shields, armour, and wadded clothes. (ENI Library)

dependent upon the strength of his unit. He was assisted by one or more *kumedans* and *mahzors* (at an approximate rate of one *kumedan* per 70 to 300–plus men, and one *mahzor* per two to eight *kumedans*). Other *derah* staff comprised a *vakil* (the *sardar*'s agent, who liaised with the government), a *nishanchi*, a *dhownsa nawaz* (chief drummer), a *harkara*, a *daftri* (writer), one or more *munshis*, a *mutassadi*, and several drummers, flag bearers, time-keepers, and *granthis*.

Although the *derahs* were independent units and there was no overall *Ghorchurra* commander, in 1822 the smallest of them were grouped together into larger units which were placed under the command of distinguished *sardars*. This process continued throughout the 1830s so that by 1845 there were just 17 *derahs*. However, this consolidation was principally an administrative measure, and the constituent *derahs* of which such units were composed remained largely autonomous in practice.

THE ARTILLERY

At the end of the 18th century only the strongest *misls* had possessed artillery, which, with a few exceptions, usually took the form of light camel-mounted swivel guns called *zamburaks* ('wasps') or *shutarnáls* ('camel-barrels'). These had a calibre of an inch or so and fired shot weighing about a pound. However, when Ranjit Singh came to power he was fortunate enough to inherit a battery of six field guns, commanded by an Afghan named Ghaus Khan. Recognizing the importance of a powerful artillery arm, Ranjit took every opportunity to accumulate more guns as quickly as possible, and by 1808 he had already amassed some 35–40 pieces, in addition to about 100 *zamburaks*. Captured forts and towns were an early source of guns, but by as early as 1807 Ranjit had established the first of several foundries in Lahore. By the 1830s he was employing technology and guidance provided by the EIC to mass-produce copies of the British guns presented to him as diplomatic gifts; these home-made pieces were occasionally rough, but always serviceable.

As first organized in 1804, the artillery was subdivided into three parts: the *topkhana kalan* (heavy guns), *topkhana khurd* (light guns), and *zamburkhana* (swivels), each being the responsibility of a separate official called a *darogha* (superintendent). This arrangement evolved into a distinct artillery corps in 1810, when Ghaus Khan was appointed *darogha-i-topkhana*. This corps was called the *Topkhana-i-khas*, or sometimes the *Topkhana-i-mubarik*.

The heavy guns were now classified as *gavi* (bullock-drawn), and the lighter guns as *aspi* (horse-drawn). In 1811 a single *derah* or battery of horse artillery was added, commanded by Mazhar Ali Beg. There were 39 guns in all, of which 17 were *gavi* and six *aspi*; five of the balance constituted the horse artillery battery, and the remaining 11 were attached to six *Fauj-i-ain* infantry battalions at the rate of – usually – two guns per battalion. In addition, there were six mortars (*ghubaras*) and 86 *zamburaks*, organized into two separate *derahs*. Further guns and *zamburaks* were to be found in the kingdom's various forts.

The Sikhs' largest guns were Mughal pieces dating from the 18th century. This one, engraved to somewhat exaggerated proportions for the *Illustrated London News*, is 'Fateh Jang', surrendered to the British in 1846 (all Sikh guns were individually named). A similar piece, capable of firing 84lb shot, is still to be seen outside Lahore Museum.

In 1814 the first horse artillery battery, by now consisting of six guns, was transferred to the *Fauj-i-ain*, and a second, of 15 guns, was raised under the command of Ilahi Bakhsh. Ghaus Khan died the same year and was succeeded as overall commander of the artillery by Misr Diwan Chand, while command of the *Topkhana-i-khas* passed to Ghaus Khan's son, Sultan Mahmud Khan. Possibly associated with Ghaus Khan's demise was the reorganization of the artillery in 1814 into horse artillery batteries (*topkhana aspi*), bullock batteries (*topkhana gavi*), elephant batteries (*topkhana fili*, particularly useful in hill country), and *zamburak*-armed camel batteries (*topkhana shutri*). By 1821 there were five horse artillery batteries attached to the *Fauj-i-ain*, increasing to six by 1823 and seven by 1826. These comprised 74 guns at the latter date, plus 25 more – a mixture of 6-pdrs and 8pdrs – attached to the infantry battalions. The number of *zamburak* batteries had meanwhile increased to two by 1819 and four by 1826.

Misr Diwan Chand died in 1825 and was succeeded by his brother Sukh Dial, who was removed from office for incompetence after just a couple of years. Overall command of the artillery then passed to Sultan Mahmud Khan, who remained in charge until April 1837, when he was dismissed for excessive drinking and replaced by *Sardar* Lehna Singh Majithia.

The dismissal of Sukh Dial in 1827 was accompanied by further reorganization. Artillery *derahs* were now reclassified as 'mixed batteries' (*topkhana jinsi*), composed of bullock- and horse-drawn guns and howitzers; horse-artillery batteries; and *zamburkhana* or swivel batteries. In addition the *Topkhana-i-khas* was broken down into individual batteries and attached to the *Fauj-i-ain*. Finally, the practice of assigning guns to individual infantry battalions was theoretically abandoned, the guns being gathered together and formed into a separate corps. In 1831, however, Claude Wade recorded all infantry battalions as still having two guns attached to them, so this last reform was apparently slow to be implemented. In 1828 there were four *jinsi* batteries, seven *aspi*, and five *zamburkhana*, totalling 130 guns, 280 swivels, and 3,778 men. The elephant-drawn heavy artillery was brigaded alongside the *jinsi*.

1831: Claude Court's reforms

The next phase of reorganization took place in 1831 under the guidance of Claude Auguste Court, whom Ranjit Singh held 'in the greatest esteem'. He had been employed in 1827 specifically for the improvement of the artillery, but it had taken several years (and a demonstration of British artillery expertise, at a meeting with the Governor-General, William Bentinck) to bring home to Ranjit the need for dramatic reform. Court then introduced French gun drill and words of command in place of the British system previously imitated. He translated a French manual into Persian to help in training the gunners, and oversaw the mass-production of guns on a much increased scale. He also taught the Sikhs how to cast shells (1832) and manufacture fuses (1833).

With the restructuring of the *Fauj-i-ain* into brigades in 1835, the artillery metamorphosed into its final form. A horse-drawn battery, or occasionally two, was attached to each brigade, while the *jinsi* batteries were consolidated as a separate corps under the direct command of Sultan Mahmud Khan (and later Lehna Singh Majithia). The *zamburak* batteries, meanwhile, were increased in quantity by being reduced in size, and were attached to the *Ghorchurras*. The *East India & Colonial Magazine* lists Sikh ordnance at about this date as comprising 58 horse-drawn guns, 135 'foot artillery' (i.e. *jinsi*) guns, nine mortars, and 314 camel-swivels, the last being organized into eight *derahs*, of 150, 40, 30, 30, 20, 19, 15, and 10 pieces respectively. In addition there were 107 guns in the kingdom's forts. These figures doubtless include *Jagirdari Fauj* guns as well as those of the *Fauj-i-ain*.

Rapid expansion, 1839–45

At Ranjit Singh's death in 1839 the regular artillery totalled 192 guns and some 4,500 gunners, organized in 14 batteries; but fortress guns and those in the possession of the *jagirdars* may have raised the total to as high as 350–400 pieces. In addition there were about 280 *zamburaks* with the regular army, and about the same number again were available from the *jagirdars* and fortresses.

Under Ranjit's successors the size of the artillery increased dramatically, and by 1845 it had doubled. When Maharaja Sher Singh died in 1843 there were 232 guns and 6,050 gunners; under Raja Hira Singh these figures increased to 282 guns, 300 swivels, and 8,280 gunners; and by 1845 – when the number of horse-artillery batteries reached 32 – there were 381

Examples of what their British captors subsequently christened the 'Sutlej Guns'. These highly ornate bronze 6pdrs, decorated with steel, brass, copper and mother-of-pearl, were captured at Ferozeshah, Aliwal and elsewhere during the First Sikh War, and at Gujerat in 1849. Surviving examples can be seen at the Woolwich Rotunda; at Fort Nelson near Portsmouth, Hampshire; in the Queen's Own Royal West Kent regimental museum at Maidstone, Kent; and at McKee Barracks in Dublin. Such handsome pieces were not typical of Sikh artillery, however; guns were more often plain, or else bore no more than a Persian inscription, and were mounted on infamously rickety carriages 'made of unseasoned wood, and of all fashions, after the fancy of the carpenters attached to Brigades'. Sikh guns fired round shot, chain shot, canister, grape, and shells. The round shot was made of iron, brass or zinc, crudely hammered into shape, or sometimes of stone or even wood. The shells were mostly of brass, copper, pewter or lead and, being loaded with no more than powder, were described by the British as 'harmless' or even 'useless'. (Norman Swales)

guns, 388 swivels, and over 11,500 gunners. All of these figures exclude fortress guns and those of the *jagirdars*; Cunningham estimated in July 1844 that the *Fauj-i-ain* and *Jagirdari Fauj* together could field 552 guns and 995 swivels, the *Fauj-i-qilajat* a further 505 guns and 1,428 swivels. However, the vast increase in the number of guns available for field service was more apparent than real, since very few of these were new, many being old pieces 'taken out of forts, furnished up, and placed on field carriages'.

Battery organization & composition

Batteries or *derahs* were named after their commanding officers and were of no fixed size. By about the end of Ranjit Singh's reign *jinsi* batteries generally consisted of 10–30 guns (though some had 40 or more), while *aspi* batteries had between five and ten, the ideal apparently being eight. Of the 32 *aspi* batteries recorded in 1845, 14 had two to seven guns, four had eight to ten, and 11 had 11–15 guns. For tactical purposes batteries were subdivided into sections of two guns, but for administrative purposes a section was considered to comprise one gun and limber and one ammunition wagon and limber. The battery was commanded by a *kumedan* (later a colonel and a *kumedan*), assisted by an *adjutan* and a *mahzor*. The highest artillery rank was general, of whom there were four by 1845.

The guns of *aspi* batteries were 3pdrs to 6pdrs, while *jinsi* batteries comprised 6½pdrs to 12pdrs. Heavier guns such as 18pdrs and 24pdrs, plus mortars and most howitzers, were nominally considered siege artillery (*kalan*), but could also be found in use on the battlefield. Indeed, despite Ranjit Singh's attempts to standardize calibres, the majority of Sikh batteries seem to have included guns of sundry shapes and sizes mixed together side by side, as can be seen from the returns of guns captured by the British during the Sikh Wars.

For instance, at the battle of Mudki (18 December 1845), the British captured six 12pdrs, four 9pdrs, three 6pdrs, one 3pdr, and one 6½pdr howitzer. The 72 pieces captured three days later at Ferozeshah comprised one 32pdr, one 24pdr, seven 18pdrs, one 15pdr, four 12pdrs, one 11pdr, four 10pdrs, 18 x 9pdrs, 13 x 8pdrs, three 7pdrs, seven 6pdrs, and seven 3pdrs, plus three howitzers (one each 9pdr, 24pdr and 42pdr), and two mortars (one 10in and one 24pdr). Full analysis of the total of 252 guns captured in the First Sikh War revealed them to be of as many as 96 different types.

Each gun of every battery was the responsibility of a *jamadar* assisted by a *havildar* and a *naik*. There were between eight and 11 gunners (*golandaz*), and five to seven non-combatants (*beldars*, *mistris*, *saqqas*, etc.) per gun. Other non-combatants included the usual *munshi*, *mutassadi*, *granthi*, flag-bearers, time-keepers and the like, plus several trumpeters (replaced by buglers in *jinsi* batteries). The total establishment of a ten-gun battery was about 250 soldiers

An engraving from the *Illustrated London News* showing a parade of bullock-drawn and elephant-drawn *jinsi* and heavy artillery surrendered to the British by the Treaty of Lahore at the conclusion of the First Sikh War.

and non-combatants. In fact, approximately half of all artillerymen were non-combatants: about 40 per cent of these were bullock-drivers, 25 per cent or more grooms, and 8 per cent smiths, carpenters, wheelwrights and the like.

Each gun and wagon of a *jinsi* battery was drawn by bullocks, camels or cart-horses, while *kalan* guns were often drawn by elephants. A single heavy gun might require up to 80 or 100 bullocks to move it. In a horse-drawn battery there were six or eight horses per gun and limber, and about the same number for the ammunition wagon. More usually, however, the latter was drawn by bullocks and camels (probably on grounds of availability), even though this compromised the battery's mobility, amounting, as Henry Lawrence put it, to 'tying up one leg of a man going to run a race'. Pack camels were sometimes employed to carry the ammunition in lieu of wagons.

Zamburak batteries continued to be of very flexible proportions. Of the six existing in 1845, two were of 40 guns, while the other four consisted of 52, 71, 80, and 105 guns. The number of gunners per battery was 61 and 73 for the two 40-gun units, and 76, 101, 127, and 146 men respectively for the others – a ratio of approximately three men per two swivel guns. A newspaper report of 1838 tells us that *zamburkhana* gunners were 'richly dressed in long scarlet coats, and their housings are of the same colour. Each... is armed with sword and pistols.' When present on a battlefield, camel swivels were positioned on the flanks.

Sundry visitors recorded adverse comments even as late as 1843 – that Sikh artillery practice was 'infamously bad' and 'very unskilful'; but in 1845–49 the Sikh artillery proved itself, in the words of one English eye-witness, 'the most effective branch of their service, working with great rapidity, and firing with almost as much precision and regularity as the British'. Another records that 'the Sikhs fired their guns in the ratio of thrice to our twice, which multiplies most fearfully the battering power of artillery, and raises the calibre of a six into a nine-pounder. At the Battle of Ferozeshah, the Sikh guns were served with extraordinary rapidity and precision.' The destructive power of their guns was further increased by the fact that they were generally heavier in metal than their British counterparts (a Sikh 4pdr, for instance, was as heavy as a British 6pdr), which meant that they could use double charges of powder, grape and shot.

THE FEUDAL ARMY – *JAGIRDARI FAUJ*

The *Jagirdari Fauj* consisted of contingents provided by the kingdom's nobility, who gave their allegiance in return for assignments of land (*jagirs*). These varied considerably in size. The smallest *jagirs*, held by ordinary *sardars*, were worth about Rs 2,000–3,000 to the grantee himself (this representing his personal allowance), in addition to the revenue necessary to maintain a contingent of troops. Those of middle size, worth Rs 20,000–40,000, were held by *sardaran-i-namdar* ('*sardars* of repute' or 'leading chiefs'); while the very largest, worth Rs 100,000 or more, were held by court favourites and members of the royal family.

The *jagirdar*, as the recipient was called, undertook to provide a specific number of men whenever called upon, the size of his contingent being specified in the deed of grant. According to William Moorcroft and John Lawrence, in Ranjit Singh's time one horseman was supposed to be provided per Rs 500 of land held, 'besides being ready with other fighting men in an emergency'; but this scale was not always adhered to. The cost of maintaining the contingent seems usually to have involved about half of the *jagir*'s revenue (which took the form of taxes, fines and gifts from the *jagirdar*'s tenants), but where it required more the *jagirdar* was sometimes assigned additional land or a cash stipend by the government. The pay of the *jagirdar*'s troopers was set out in the deed of grant in the case of smaller *jagirs*, but the most powerful *jagirdars* set their own rates of pay. Most *Jagirdari* cavalrymen nevertheless received much the same wages (about Rs 250–300 per annum), which often took the form of a sub-let portion of the *jagir*. Most *Jagirdari* soldiers were kinsmen and clansmen of the *jagirdar*.

The *jagirdars*' contingents thus varied in size from a handful of men up to several thousand, but in the field they were customarily organized into *derahs* of some 300–500 each, and up to six *derahs* might be collected together to form the equivalent of a brigade. John Lawrence considered the *Jagirdari* 'in a great degree both useless and expensive, invariably ill-paid, half-armed and unorganized'; so it comes as no surprise to find that they were employed mainly for minor operations of no particular importance. Occasionally a money payment was levied from the *jagirdar* instead of men, when his troops had not been called up for so long that there were doubts regarding their effectiveness. In addition, Ranjit Singh's successors sometimes excused *jagirdars* from providing their military contingents on payment of a fine.

When the *jagirdar* died, control of his lands and troops reverted to the state, the cavalry being transferred to the *Misldar Sowaran* (see above – part of the *Ghorchurra Fauj*). After his affairs had been settled, however, there was a reasonable chance that the *jagir* would be re-assigned to his heirs, who would then resume responsibility for the maintenance of the *jagir*'s contingent of troops.

The *jagirdar* was expected to attend a review of the *Khalsa* army at Lahore or Amritsar with all his troops once a year – customarily at the beginning of October – so that they could be inspected. Every soldier was required to attend on such occasions, on pain of fines. In order to avoid fraud

Matchlock-armed Sikh irregular infantryman at the time of the First Sikh War: an engraving from the *Illustrated London News*. (ENI Library)

the *jagirdars* had to submit an exhaustive descriptive roll (*chihra*) of their men and horses to the state archive. Men who attempted to defraud the government ran the risk of forfeiting their *jagirs*, and were heavily fined (on one famous occasion in 1828 one of Ranjit Singh's most famous generals, Hari Singh Nalwa, was fined Rs 200,000 for maintaining only 450 horsemen instead of the required 600).

The *chihra* listed each individual's name (as well as the names of his father and grandfather), home town, caste, height, complexion, colour of eyes, distinguishing features, scars, and so on. As his career progressed, details of promotions and demotions, pay increases and reductions, fines and transfers were added to the archive. The colour and markings of his horse were also given, as were details of replacement horses when these had to be substituted. All *Jagirdari* horses were given an official brand to aid identification.

Jagirdari infantry and artillery

Minor *jagirdars* were usually expected to provide no more than cavalry, but by the mid-1830s royal princes and leading chiefs – and in particular those whose estates consisted of hill country, such as the Dogra rajas – were also expected to maintain units of infantry and artillery. The infantry comprised both regulars and irregulars, the latter being a mixture of garrison troops and *bandukchis*, 'matchlock men' (some of whom, despite their name, were actually armed with no more than a spear or sword, and all of whom were little better than armed camp-followers).

Jagirdari regular infantry were trained, organized, uniformed, and armed exactly like those of the *Fauj-i-ain*, some (notably those of Gulab Singh and Suchet Singh) even having foreign instructors. Shahamat Ali, who was in the Punjab in 1839, credits the *Jagirdari* with nine battalions of regular infantry at that date, but their numbers increased considerably following Ranjit's death. Smyth was of the opinion that there were 25 battalions in about 1843, of which as many as 21 had been raised by the Dogra chiefs. Most of the *sardars* required to field such troops had to maintain just one or two battalions, but Gulab Singh maintained as many as eight by this time, and his nephew Hira Singh four. Like the state regulars, *Jagirdari* battalions were organized into companies. One battalion for which details survive comprised five companies, each consisting of a *subedar*, *jamadar*, four *havildars*, four *naiks*, two drummers, and about a hundred men.

The *jagirdars* were at first forbidden to possess cannon, but from the mid-1820s onwards the more important of them might be called upon to provide artillery in addition to their contingents of horse and foot. In 1825, for example, *Diwan* Kirpa Ram provided 100 *zamburaks* and five guns in addition to 2,300 cavalry and 500 infantry; and in 1835, the Dogra rajas are said to have maintained 'six 9pdr, six 6pdr horse artillery guns, four mortars, four howitzers, two 3pdr mountain guns, 22 pieces in all, besides some camel guns'. In 1843–44 Nihal Singh Ahluwalia fielded 1,900 foot (three battalions), 1,500 horse, 15 guns, and 25 *zamburaks*. According to Shahamat Ali, the leading

A Sikh *sardar* in typical costume, sketched by Osborne in 1838. Note the characteristic black *kalga* or heron feather in his turban. (ENI Library)

(continued on page 33)

1: *Jagirdari* horseman, 1799–1849
2: Irregular infantryman, c.1815
3: Early regular infantryman, c.1810–20

A

1: *Fauj-i-ain* officer, 1830s
2: General Jean-Francois Allard, c.1835
3: Maharaja Ranjit Singh, c.1835

B

1: *Fauj-i-ain* sepoy, 1820s
2: *Fauj-i-ain naik,* 1830s–40s
3: *Fauj-i-khas* sepoy, 1830s–40s

1

2

3

C

1: *Fauj-i-ain* sepoy, winter dress, 1830s
2: *Fauj-i-khas* Purbia sepoy, 1830s–40s
3: *Fauj-i-ain* sepoy, summer dress, 1830s

1

2

3

D

1: *Aspi* artilleryman, 1825–46
2: *Jinsi* artilleryman, 1825–46
3: *Aspi* Muslim artilleryman, c.1840

1: *Fauj-i-ain* cuirassier, c.1839
2: Sowar, 2nd Lancers, 1838
3: Dragoon, c.1840

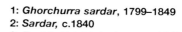

1: *Ghorchurra sardar*, 1799–1849
2: *Sardar*, c.1840
3: *Fauj-i-qilajat* infantryman, 1840s

G

1: *Ghorchurra Khas* sowar, 1838
2 & 3: *Akalis*, 1799–1849

H

A stand of traditional Sikh arms, from Osborne's *The Court and Camp of Runjeet Singh*. From top, a re-curved bow, quiver, powder horn, helmet with mail curtain, shield, long matchlock musket, axe, sword; vambraces of mixed plate and mail construction, and *char-aina* breastplate; and a *katar* or 'punch dagger'. (ENI Library)

jagirdars could field a total of 87 horse-drawn and bullock-drawn guns between them. At least some *Jagirdari* artillery contingents were organized and trained as regulars.

There were about 15,000 *Jagirdari Fauj* troops in 1808; 20,000 in 1821; 27,300 in 1831; and perhaps 50,000 at the outbreak of the First Sikh War in 1845. Their rapid increase in numbers during the anarchy following Ranjit Singh's death reflects the rise in power of the Dogra *jagirdars* and the simultaneous increase in their military might. By February 1844 the most ambitious of them, Gulab Singh of Jammu, was capable of fielding 15,500 infantry, 1,700 cavalry, and 1,035 artillerymen, with 94 guns and 250 camel swivels.

THE GARRISON ARMY – *FAUJ-I-QILAJAT*

The *Fauj-i-qilajat* was responsible for guarding the kingdom's forts, roadside guardposts, city gates and state treasuries, while an associated corps, the *Sair Jamaat*, provided local constabulary. The *Fauj-i-qilajat* was composed entirely of locally raised irregular infantry and artillery, though the most important forts (such as Attock, Kangra, Multan, Peshawar, and Srinagar) received in addition small contingents of regular troops, sometimes including cavalry.

This force had neither battalions nor companies. Instead, regardless of its size – which inevitably varied, according to circumstances and the size of the post, from just 25 men up to more than a thousand – each garrison constituted a separate, independent unit commanded by an officer holding the rank of *jamadar*. He in turn came under the orders of the fort commander, known as a *qiladar* or *thanadar*. Large garrisons might be subdivided, though only for administrative purposes, into smaller units called *baradaris* ('brotherhoods'), known by the names of their individual commanders, who usually also held the rank of *jamadar*. Garrison units were not uniformed, were 'variously armed and equipped', did not serve in the field, and were never transferred. In Ranjit Singh's reign they were paid Rs 5–7 per month, their *jamadars* receiving twice as much or a little more.

Because the kingdom's frontiers continued to expand, the size of the *Fauj-i-qilajat* steadily increased. In 1818 it comprised only about 5,000 men, including the *Sair Jamaat*. This figure had increased to 9,000 by 1821; to about 11,000 by the mid-1820s; and to 23,950 foot and 3,000 horse by 1831. In 1843 Cunningham put the strength of the *Fauj-i-qilajat* at 28,000 foot, 4,509 horse, and 1,324 artillerymen, with 505 guns and 1,428 swivels.

THE *AKALIS*

The *Akalis* or 'Immortals' (also known as *Nihangs*) were Sikh fundamentalists, dedicated to defending their faith by force of arms, while at the same time often found acting in the capacity of priests. Most foreign visitors considered them rabid fanatics, one writing that 'their fanaticism borders on insanity'. In 1830 a Sikh official described the typical *Akali* as a man 'whose body is unaffected by pain or comfort. He is a man of firm faith, sexual restraint, meditation, penance and charity, and a complete warrior. In the presence of worldly authority, he remains full of pride. Where there is the place of battle, having no fear of death, he never steps back.'

Although they were based at Anandpur and Amritsar, the *Akalis* led an itinerant lifestyle, travelling alone or in sizeable bands, depending on charity for their sustenance or else simply helping themselves to what they needed. Ranjit Singh often had to deploy troops to prevent them from terrorizing the population in this way, and several minor affrays are recorded. Yet he also gave them lands and precious gifts – perhaps in an effort to buy their loyalty, since they are reputed to have made several attempts to kill him (they disapproved of his tolerance of the British). They verbally abused him during military parades, and even pelted him with mud when they got the chance.

Their pride also rendered them a political embarrassment. They attacked a British envoy and his escort as early as 1809, and frequently raided in British-protected Sikh territory beyond the Sutlej river. It was as a step towards curbing their exuberance that, by 1818, Ranjit Singh had incorporated at least 2,000–3,000 *Akalis* (some say 4,000–5,000) into his army as an irregular corps of mounted infantry called the *Changari*.

This *Akali* is very probably a member of the corps attached to the state army; comprising four regiments, this force was called the *Changari* ('Live Coals'), and was initially commanded by a celebrated *Akali* named Phula Singh, who was killed at the battle of Naushehra in 1823. In 1838 these fanatics were recorded to 'still wear their odd coarse blue dresses and carry their own arms – sharpened quoits, swords, and pistols in profusion'. His noticeably ill-conditioned mount is for transport only – the *Changari* were essentially mounted infantry. (ENI Library)

Although they would not submit to military discipline or training, and insisted on pursuing traditional Sikh tactics rather than the new-fangled European system introduced by Ranjit Singh, the *Akalis'* extreme bravery rendered them ideal for employment in desperate enterprises, and their courage was pivotal in the Sikh victories at Multan in 1818 and Naushehra in 1823. However, such employment had considerably reduced their numbers by the 1830s, which

Quoits (*chakkars*), a characteristic weapon of the *Akalis*, were thin iron rings of various diameters (most often about 6–12in) with a sharpened outer edge. Some were decoratively engraved; this silver-inlaid example (both sides are shown, as left & right halves) was made in Lahore following the British occupation of the Punjab. Foreign visitors describe quoits as being spun around the forefinger before being launched at the enemy (as portrayed in this picture from Capt Mundy's *Pen and Pencil Sketches* of 1832); but modern-day exponents hold them between thumb and forefinger and throw them either over arm from behind the head, or back-handed across the body from the left side, like a 'frisbee'. It was claimed that a thrown quoit could slice through neck or limb at 60–80 yards, but this is doubtful. Significantly, not a single British soldier is recorded as being wounded by a quoit during the Sikh Wars.

Native painting of an *Akali*, dated 1833. He carries a war quoit on the usual dark blue *dastar bunga* turban – here of uncharacteristically modest proportions – with a light blue tunic trimmed white, pale yellow shorts and decorated red slippers. His slung shield, sword scabbard, and the powder horn and bullet pouches at his waist, are also shown as red. (Tony Paul)

was doubtless Ranjit's underlying intention – since they were his most unruly subjects, observed one British officer, he 'endeavoured to use them up as fast as possible'. Their numbers were further diminished during the fighting which followed Sher Singh's death in 1843; they suffered additional heavy losses in the First Sikh War, notably at Sobraon (10 February 1846), after which little more was heard of them.

RECRUITMENT & COMPOSITION

The Sikhs' deep-rooted contempt for foot-soldiers, and their reluctance to submit to the drill, discipline, and uniforms of a European-style army, meant that initially few Punjabis volunteered for service in Ranjit's regular infantry force. Instead, his first recruits – including many EIC deserters – were largely Purbias (Hindustani Hindus and Muslims), and to a lesser extent Rajputs, Ranghors (Muslim Rajputs), Afghans, Najibs (men from the Saharanpur district) and Gurkhas. These elements continued to predominate until about 1813.

However, since Ranjit's aim was to create a truly national army, he did all he could to encourage Sikhs and other Punjabis to enlist. His instructors persuaded men to attend drill by means of gifts, lavish meals and cash prizes; and Ranjit himself set an example by personally participating in infantry drill, wearing 'the unaccustomed dress of a British foot-soldier'. By such means the Sikhs' traditional prejudices were slowly overcome, and by February 1812 the first two Sikh battalions had been created. From 1818 onwards Punjabi recruitment steadily increased, and during the 1820s the Purbia Hindus who had constituted the majority of regular infantry in the earlier part of Ranjit's reign were gradually displaced.

By 1839 the majority of regular infantrymen were probably Sikhs; but the political turmoil which followed Ranjit Singh's death that year led to the adoption in 1841 of a deliberate policy of enlisting in their place Dogras (Rajput hillmen from Dougar Desh in Jammu) whenever possible. Even so, in the mid-1840s the greater part of the regular infantry still consisted of Sikhs, the balance being largely Dogras, Hindus, Muslims and Gurkhas. In 1844 it was estimated that of the entire army, 60 per cent were Sikh and 20 per cent Hindu. Of the regular infantry battalion commanders recorded that year, 36 were Sikh, 16 Hindu, three Muslim, and five European, while the regular cavalry regiments were commanded by three Sikhs, two Muslims, and one European.

The *Jagirdari* and the largest part of the *Ghorchurras* consisted of Sikhs and Rajputs, but almost every other Punjabi ethnic group was also represented in their ranks. The clan and family nature of their enlistment inevitably meant that these served in self-contained rather

Table 2: Composition of *Fauj-i-ain units*, 1844

(As recorded by J.D.Cunningham)

Commander	Men	Infantry Bns	Cavalry Regts	Light guns	Field guns	Fortress guns
Sardar Tej Singh	Sikhs	4	1	10	–	–
Gen Pertab Singh Pattiwala	Sikhs	3	–	–	–	–
Gen Jawala Singh	*infantry* Sikhs; *artillery* Sikhs & Muslims	2	–	4	–	–
Sheikh Imam-ud-di	Muslims	3	–	4	–	–
Sardar Lehna Singh Majithia	*inf & most arty* Sikhs	2	–	10	3	2
Gen Bisham Singh	Muslims & few Sikhs	2	–	3	–	–
Gen Gulab Singh Puhuvindhia	*inf* Muslims; *arty* Sikhs & Muslims	3	–	14	–	–
Gen Mahtab Singh Majithia	*inf* Sikhs; *cav* mixed; *arty* Sikhs & Muslims	4	1	12	–	–
Gen Gurdut Singh Majithia	chiefly Sikhs	3	–	–	–	–
Col John Holmes	*inf* chiefly Sikhs, *arty* Sikhs & Muslims	1	–	10	–	–
Gen Dhaunkal Singh	Hindustanis & few Sikhs	2	–	–	–	–
Gen Cortlandt *(discharged)*	*inf* Sikhs & Hindustanis; *arty* Sikhs & Muslims	2	–	10	–	–
Shaikh Ghulam Muhi-ud-Din	Sikhs?; *arty* Sikhs & Muslims	1	–	6	8	–
Diwan Ajudhia Prashad	Sikhs; *arty* Sikhs & Muslims	4	2	12	22	–
Gen Gulab Singh Calcuttawala *(deceased)*	Sikhs	4	1	16	–	–
Diwan Jodha Ram	Sikhs, Muslims & Dogras	4	1	12	3	–
Gen Kahn Singh Man	Sikhs & Muslims	4	–	10	–	–
Sardar Nihal Singh Ahluwalia	Sikhs & Muslims; *arty* chiefly Muslims	1	–	4	11	–
Diwan Sawan Mal	Muslims, some Sikhs	3	–	6	–	40
Raja Hira Singh	Dogras, some Muslims	2	1	–	3	5
Raja Gulab Singh	Dogras, some Muslims	3	–	15	–	40
Raja Suchet Singh *(deceased)*	Dogras, some Muslims	2	1	4	–	10
Capt Kuldip Singh	Gurkhas	1	–	–	–	–
Kumedan Bhag Singh	Sikhs & Muslims	–	–	6	–	–
Kumedan Shev Prashad	Sikhs & Muslims	–	–	8	–	–
Misr Lal Singh	Sikhs & Muslims	–	–	10	–	–
Sardar Kishan Singh	Muslims & Hindustanis	–	–	–	–	2
Gen Kishan Singh	Sikhs & Muslims	–	–	22	–	–
Sardar Sham Singh Atariwala	Sikhs & Muslims	–	–	–	10	–
Mian Prithi Singh	chiefly Muslims	–	–	–	56	–
Gen Mahwa Singh	Sikhs & Muslims	–	–	10	10	–
Col Amir Chand	chiefly Muslims	–	–	–	10	–
Kumedan Mazhar Ali Beg	Muslims & Hindustanis	–	–	10	–	–
Jawahar Mal Mistr	Muslims & few Sikhs	–	–	–	20	12
Kumedan Sukhu Singh	Sikhs, some Hindustanis	–	–	–	–	10
Miscellaneous garrison guns		–	–	–	–	50
Totals		60	8	228	156	171

than mixed units – i.e., the troops of Sikh *jagirdars* were Sikhs and those of Muslim *jagirdars* Muslims. During Ranjit Singh's reign approximately 10 per cent of irregular cavalry were Muslims. The regular cavalry, on the other hand, were a mixture of Sikhs, Rajputs, Muslims, and Dogras, though here too Sikhs predominated. Wade wrote in April 1827 that the Dragoons were mostly Sikhs, while the Lancers were 'chiefly Pathans from Hindustan' but included two troops of Sikhs.

Though only small numbers of Muslims were to be found in the cavalry and infantry, they predominated in the artillery from the outset, and even as late as 1845 they constituted some 60 per cent of all artillerymen. The overall commander of the artillery and more than half the battery commanders were also Muslims. Initially most artillerymen were Hindustani Muslims, but these were gradually replaced by Punjabi Muslims. The reason for the relative dearth of Sikh artillerymen, in the opinion of the French mercenary officer Court, was that Ranjit Singh was 'somewhat reluctant' to hire Sikh gunners, 'because he feared their unruliness'.

Rajputs were found throughout the army, including the *Ghorchurras* and the *Fauj-i-qilajat*. There were three or four battalions of Rajput regular infantry as early as 1825, but in the 1830s and 1840s – especially after the Dogra rajas gained ascendancy following Ranjit's death – their numbers increased dramatically. By about 1842 there were reportedly some 10,000 Dogra Rajput troops.

Gurkhas were found only in the *Fauj-i-ain*. Ranjit Singh had begun to recruit them in about 1809, having been impressed by their fighting prowess during his invasion of Kangra. Not all of his so-called Gurkhas were genuine, however: Osborne records Ranjit telling him in 1838 that 'he found difficulty' in keeping their numbers up, and afterwards ascertained that in reality 'not above one man in twenty is a real Goorkha', the majority being hillmen from Kashmir. Ranjit's first Gurkha battalion existed before 1815, in which year a second was raised; in 1845 these two battalions totalled some 1,500 men.

It can be seen, therefore, that the 'Sikh' army was actually a multi-ethnic force embracing a wide variety of peoples and religions. This was only occasionally problematic – for instance, on the occasion of the battle of Chuch, when the Muslim commander of Ranjit's artillery refused to fire on his Afghan co-religionists. On the whole, Ranjit succeeded in minimizing the risk of ethnic, religious or political tensions by indiscriminately mixing men of different backgrounds in his units. This also prevented any one particular group from attaining a dominant position. There were, nevertheless, numerous 'pure' units – Sikh, Purbia, Muslim, Rajput, Dogra, Hindustani, and Gurkha – in all three arms, and this trend increased with the passage of time, especially under Ranjit's successors.

* * *

The military basis of Sikh culture meant that once initial reservations had been overcome, the recruitment of troops for the *Fauj-i-ain* presented no real difficulties. Military service was popular, and the conditions of service were attractive, with the possibility of rapid promotion and the promise of high (if often delayed) pay. When it came to raising his regular infantry, therefore, Ranjit Singh was able to be selective. He personally chose every recruit, picking men who were aged 17–24 and stood at least 5ft 8in tall. Later, enlistment could start at the age of 15 and continue up to 65 years. In the period 1839–49, however, recruitment was often delegated to individual senior officers and *sardars*

Typical Sikh upper-class dress of the 1830s is shown in this painting made in December 1838 by Emily Eden, of two members of the retinue of Ranjit Singh's son and short-lived successor to the throne, Kharak Singh. (ENI Library)

rather than being controlled by the state. Consequently it became less selective and subject to fewer controls, officers and *sardars* alike occasionally enlisting additional men without government approval.

Most regular soldiers were enlisted in the rank of private, but some – usually either the kinsmen of court favourites, or men with military experience in the ranks of the EIC or the army of a neighbouring state – were recruited as NCOs or officers. Most officers were recruited amongst the sons and kinsmen of *sardars*. Few had any previous military experience, many were illiterate, and some were utterly incompetent: indeed, the poor quality of its officer corps was to prove the *Khalsa* army's most severe handicap during the Sikh Wars of 1845–49.

THE DEMISE OF THE SIKH ARMY

Treaties signed with the British from 1806 onwards had frustrated Ranjit Singh's plans to expand his state eastwards beyond the Sutlej or southwards into Sind. Thereafter, despite the eventual signing of a 'treaty of perpetual friendship' with the Governor-General of India in 1831, an element of wariness and mutual suspicion gradually crept into Anglo-Sikh relations. Ranjit was nevertheless astute enough to maintain a friendly posture towards his powerful neighbour, and even sent troops to participate in a 'demonstration' in support of the British invasion of Afghanistan in 1839. At his death in June of that same year the *Khalsa* army probably stood at some 75,000–80,000 men in all, of whom perhaps 35,000–40,000 were regulars.

Without his strong hand to guide it, Ranjit's kingdom subsequently fell prey to court rivalries and rapidly spiralled into anarchy. His immediate successor was his eldest son Kharak Singh; but he died (possibly of poison) less than 18 months later. He was succeeded in 1841 – with the support of the army – by his half-brother Sher Singh, who was assassinated in September 1843. Ranjit's eighth son, Dalip Singh, was then proclaimed Maharaja, although, since he was a minor, royal authority became vested in the hands of Ranjit's widow, Rani Jindan, and her lover, Raja Lal Singh.

Even before Ranjit's death, however, much of the real power in the country had already devolved into the hands of the ambitious Dogra brothers Dhyan Singh (the prime minister), Gulab Singh (Raja of Jammu), and Suchet Singh (Raja of Samba and Ramnagar). After 1839 these noblemen became entirely independent of central authority, and engineered the murder of several of Ranjit's heirs and ministers in a deliberate policy of family aggrandisement – although Dhyan (d.1843) and Suchet (d.1844)

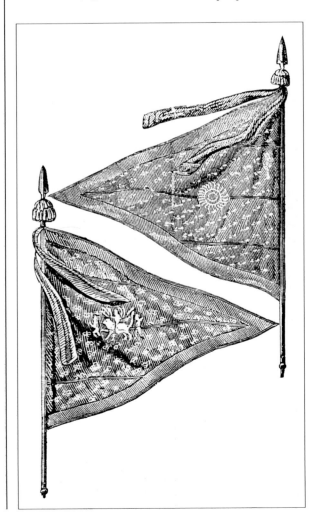

Flags captured by the British at the battles of Sobraon (top) and Ferozeshah, as portrayed in the *Illustrated London News* of 19 December 1846. Most Sikh flags were triangular, only the French-style flags of the elite *Fauj-i-khas* being square. Eyewitnesses record seeing black, yellow, red, and green flags with variously coloured borders and devices during the First and Second Sikh Wars. Note the three horizontal bands, the repeat patterning of the fields, and the central motifs; and see also pages 44–45.

themselves fell victim to the resultant anarchy. It was Dhyan's son Hira Singh who, after a half-hearted attempt to become Maharaja himself, enthroned Dalip Singh and became prime minister – only to be charged with treason by Rani Jindan, for dismissing some 300 army officers in order to cut costs. Fleeing from Lahore, Hira Singh was killed in December 1844.

The one stable power amidst this turmoil was the army, which – increasingly aware of its political importance – came to regard itself as the only true representative of Sikh aspirations. Anyone seeking to attain political dominance had no choice but to solicit the army's support, which was invariably secured by an increase in its pay. Army support for Sher Singh in January 1841, for instance, was bought by the guarantee of a monthly pay increase for the infantrymen from Rs 8 to Rs 12. In December 1844 Rani Jindan and her brother Jawahar Singh promised to increase infantry pay to Rs 14; and in January 1845 another of Ranjit's sons, Pashaura Singh, promised infantrymen Rs 15 and irregular cavalrymen not less than Rs 40, plus a gold bracelet worth Rs 100 for every soldier, if the army would support his own abortive attempt to seize the throne.

Unsurprisingly under such circumstances, with the *Khalsa* unwittingly following the example of the Praetorian Guard during one of Imperial Rome's more decadent episodes, government control of the army steadily weakened. Men took leave whenever they liked, discipline deteriorated, and training all but ceased. Hira Singh was briefly able to reintroduce regular parades in 1844, but by early 1845 it was recorded that 'exercise and drill were out of use', and a number of parade grounds were subsequently ploughed up and sown with crops. In addition, many

Three *Khalsa* sepoys: a Sikh, a Muslim, and a Gurkha – see discussion of last in commentary to Plate D2. The native paintings on which these engraved images were based must have been collected during 1838–49; they were published in Honigberger's book in 1852. Table 2 gives some details of the mixing of ethnic groups within Sikh commands. (ENI Library)

SEPAHEE

MOOSELMAN SEPAHEE

SEPAHEE

Kharak Singh's successor, his half-brother Sher Singh, depicted in 1838 wearing complete armour; compare with Plate G1. Although his succession was supported by the army, Sher Singh lasted little longer than his predecessor before himself falling victim to the anarchy of the early 1840s. From Osborne's *The Court and Camp of Runjeet Singh*. (ENI Library)

officers were murdered during mutinies in support of one or another political faction, and the rest were subjected to methodical harassment and intimidation.

The army was only saved from a complete breakdown by its *panchayats*, created in 1841. These were committees of ordinary soldiers, elected to voice each unit's views and to represent its wishes and needs in negotiations with higher authorities. By imposing 'an iron discipline' of their own, such committees ensured that the army's confidence and morale never wavered even during this anarchic period. Lord Gough describes how the *panchayats* 'guided the united action of the soldiery, were able to dictate to their officers, and later on found themselves able to appear as representing the Khalsa in arms, and to dictate to the "Durbar", or Court, itself'. Army officers were thereby rendered mere figureheads, and had to humour their men if they wanted to be obeyed. Needless to say, many of the army's foreign officers found their positions untenable; most of those who did not resign were dismissed by Hira Singh in 1844.

Despite, or perhaps because of, the country's unsettled condition, the army nevertheless increased in size dramatically after 1839. Sher Singh put its strength at 120,000 men in 1842, and other estimates suggest that it had reached 145,000–150,000 by 1845. In 1842 some 50,000 of these were regulars, increasing to more than 72,000 by the outbreak of the First Sikh War in 1845.

The Sikh Wars

The British had meanwhile become increasingly concerned over the deteriorating situation in the Punjab, and had been provocatively moving men and matériel up to the frontier in anticipation of war. At the same time, elements within the Sikh court, fearful of the *Khalsa* army, advocated distracting it from further political meddling by launching a campaign into British-protected Sikh territory beyond the Sutlej. The British began assembling their troops on 6 December 1845, and the Sikh army, under the command of Tej Singh and Lal Singh, crossed the Sutlej on the 11th.

The ensuing conflict lasted just two months, with major engagements being fought at Mudki on 18 December, Ferozeshah on the 21st–22nd, Aliwal on 28 January 1846, and Sobraon on 10 February. In all but the first of these the Sikhs, doubtless recognizing from their defeat at Mudki that they were insufficiently skilled at manoeuvring in the open field, occupied fortified positions and awaited the British attacks. This enabled them to employ their superior artillery to best effect, and they were able to inflict significant casualties on the Queen's and EIC troops which faced them. At Mudki they fielded perhaps 20,000–30,000 men and 40 guns; at Ferozeshah, some 60,000 men and 120–150 guns; at

Aliwal, only 12,000 men but more than 80 guns; and at Sobraon, about 20,000 men and nearly 70 guns.

All of these battles were hard-fought affairs, the British being both impressed and surprised by the unanticipated courage and determination of their adversaries. (The *Khalsa*'s ability to inflict heavy casualties was multiplied by the unimaginative orders of the British commander, General Sir Hugh Gough, whose tactical repertoire extended no further than frontal assaults with the bayonet). Many British officers privately conceded that the battle of Ferozeshah in particular was 'a very

Henry Martens' print, published in 1849, of the 31st Foot attacking Sikh infantry and *aspi* artillery at the battle of Mudki, fought at dusk on 18 December 1845. (ENI Library)

Table 3: Growth of Sikh army, 1839–47

(From a British report, December 1847)

	Ranjit Singh	Kharak Singh	Sher Singh	Hira Singh	Jawahar Singh	Lal Singh	since Lal Singh	Dec 1847
Inf bns	35	38	45	46	63	63	34	25
men	28,723	30,954	36,458	35,627	59,846	50,343	25,111	19,572
Cav regts	10	10	12	12	13	15	9	7
men	4,665	4,665	5,782	5,790	6,235	6,207	3,887	3,682
Arty btys	14	14	22	24	33	36	20	18
men	4,250	4,250	5,947	7,105	10,747	10,132	6,505	5,907
Ghorchurras:								
paid jagirs	1,209	1,210	1,296	1,313	1,409	1,613	669	669
paid cash	9,586	10,559	13,087	14,457	17,691	19,626	12,983	6,149
Jagirdari	3,429	3,430	3,817	3,823	3,858	3,858	3,970	4,024
Sepoys attached to forts & posts	2,802	3,133	7,843	8,523	14,700	14,700	10,719	5,495
Zamburkhanas:								
btys	4	4	5	6	6	6	8	8
men	230	230	398	511	584	584	509	509
Local irregulars 'of various descriptions'	60	60	1,243	13,301	13,154	13,154	12,538	8,990
Fort garrisons:								
bns	49	45	53	42	45	45	26	25
men	10,872	13,599	15,783	13,301	13,154	13,154	12,538	8,990
'French and English officers'	15	9	9	9	2	2	2	21

The Dogra rajas, who dominated Sikh politics in the period 1839–45: (above), the brothers Gulab Singh and Dhyan Singh; (right), Suchet Singh and Dhyan's son Hira Singh. (ENI Library)

Tej Singh – considered by some of his British opponents to be 'an officer of considerable talent', but by others as 'faint-hearted' – was commander of the *Khalsa*'s regular troops from 1826, and commander-in-chief during and after the First Sikh War. (ENI Library)

desperate affair'; so uncertain was its outcome, in fact, that the Sikhs actually claimed it as a victory – if it was a British victory, then it was certainly a far from decisive one. General Gough himself admitted that, 'Never did a native army having so relatively slight an advantage in numbers fight a battle with the British in which the issue was so doubtful as at Ferozeshah.'

Despite Gough's obstinate refusal to vary his 'Tipperary tactics', however, the battle of Sobraon was a much more decisive affair, where the Sikhs reputedly admitted to the loss of as many as 13,000–14,000 men. Every gun engaged was also captured, and at least seven generals and senior *sardars* were killed. This, coupled with the army's losses in the preceding engagements, was sufficient to bring the war to an abrupt end.

By the Treaty of Lahore, signed on 9 March 1846, the kingdom became a British protectorate in all but name, with a British resident established in Lahore. The Sikhs were obliged to surrender all their territory between the Sutlej and Beas rivers, and to reduce their army to just 20,000 infantry (25 battalions of 800 men) and 12,000 cavalry. The treaty also required that the remaining 36 guns known to have been pointed at the British at Sobraon be given up. As reward for his aid in negotiating the treaty, the British recognized Gulab Singh as independent Maharaja of Jammu and Kashmir. The army was further reduced by the Treaty of Bhyrowal in December the same year, which set its strength at 15,200 regular infantry, 2,675 regular cavalry, 1,650 artillery, 3,165 *Ghorchurras*, and 4,000 *Jagirdari*.

Continuing internal opposition to British interference in Sikh affairs culminated in the murder of two British officers at Multan in April 1848. The unrest at Multan grew into a general uprising against the British-backed Lahore government, and the Second Sikh War broke out in September. Many old *Khalsa* units spontaneously re-formed to take up arms against the British, who took until November to march back into the Punjab. Other than the siege and capture of Multan there were only two battles of any consequence: at Chillianwalla on 13 January 1849, and at Gujerat on 21 February. Both sides claimed victory at Chillianwalla; but – condemned once again by Hugh Gough to blind frontal attacks – the British troops suffered such massive losses that the Viceroy, Lord Dalhousie, declared that 'a few more such victories will lose us the Empire'. At Gujerat, however, the Sikhs were decisively defeated. The wreck of the *Khalsa* army – just 16,000 men – surrendered on 14 March, giving up its remaining 41 guns. A fortnight later the British formally annexed the Punjab, deposed Maharaja Dalip Singh, and disbanded the Sikh army.

SELECT BIBLIOGRAPHY

The following are the most worthwhile English-language publications to include information on the evolution, organization, uniforms, and equipment of the Sikh army under Ranjit Singh and his successors.

Ali, Shahamat, *The Sikhs and Afghans* (1847)

Bajwa, Fauja Singh, *Military System of the Sikhs during the Period 1799–1849* (1964)

Banerjee, A.C., *The Khalsa Raj* (1985)

Barr, William, *Journal of a March from Delhi to Peasawur, and from Thence to Cabul* (1844)

Carleton, Neil, 'The Lion's Teeth: The Artillery of the Maharaja Ranjit Singh', *Soldiers of the Queen* No.109 (2002)

Chhabra, G.S., *Advanced History of the Punjab* Vol.II (1973)

Chopra, Barkat Rai, *Kingdom of the Punjab 1839–45* (1969)

Chopra, Gulshan Lall, *The Panjab as a Sovereign State 1799–1839* (1960)

Cunningham, J.D. (ed. H.L.O.Garrett), *A History of the Sikhs* (1918)

Fane, Henry Edward, *Five Years in India*, 2 vols (1842)

Gough, Charles, & Innes, Arthur D., *The Sikhs and the Sikh Wars* (1897)

Grey, C. (ed. H.L.O.Garrett), *European Adventurers of Northern India 1785 to 1849* (1929)

Griffin, Lepel, *Ranjit Singh* (1892)

Gupta, Hari Ram, *History of the Sikhs* Vol.V (1991)

Gupta, Hari Ram (ed.), *Panjab on the Eve of First Sikh War* (1956)

Hügel, Baron Charles (ed. & trans. T.B.Jervis), *Travels in Kashmir and the Panjab* (1845)

Humbley, W.W.W., *The Journal of a Cavalry Officer* (1854)

Kohli, Sita Ram, 'The Army of Maharaja Ranjit Singh', *Journal of Indian History* I–V (1921–26), & XIII–XIV (1934–35)

Lafont, Jean-Marie, *French Administrators of Maharaja Ranjit Singh* (1988)

Lafont, Jean-Marie, *Maharaja Ranjit Singh: Lord of the Five Rivers* (2002)

Lawrence, H.M.L., *Adventures of an Officer in the Service of Runjeet Singh*, 2 vols (1845)

Mackinnon, D.H. (writing as 'A Cavalry Officer'), *Military Service and Adventures in the Far East*, 2 vols (1847)

The 16th Lancers charging Sikh infantry and artillery at the battle of Aliwal, 28 January 1846. Note the artillerymen in their tall black turbans, fighting with swords in defence of their guns. An eyewitness of the First Sikh War described Sikh artillerymen as 'gigantic, their usual stature being from six feet to six feet three inches, muscular and active in proportion'. (ENI Library)

M'Gregor, W.L., *The History of the Sikhs*, 2 vols (1846)

Majumdar, B.N., 'Military System of the Sikhs', *Journal of the United Service Institution of India* LXXXX (1960)

Masson, Charles, *Narrative of Various Journeys in Balochistan, Afghanistan and the Panjab* Vol.I (1842)

Moorcroft, William, & Trebeck, George (ed. H.H. Wilson), *Travels in the Himalayan Provinces of Hindustan and the Panjab* Vol.I (1841)

Osborne, W.G., *The Court and Camp of Runjeet Sing* (1840)

Pearse, Hugh (ed.), *Soldier and Traveller: Memoirs of Alexander Gardner* (1898)

Prinsep, Henry T., *Origin of the Sikh Power in the Punjab* (1834)

'Runjeet Singh and His Army', *East India and Colonial Magazine* XVI (1838)

'Runjeet Singh's Army', *Parbury's Oriental Herald* II (1838)

'The Seikhs and their Country', *The Calcutta Review* I (1844)

Smyth, G.Carmichael, *A History of the Reigning Family of Lahore* (1847)

Steinbach, Henry, *The Punjaub: Being a Brief Account of the Country of the Sikhs* (1846)

Stronge, Susan (ed.), *The Arts of the Sikh Kingdoms* (1999)

Vigne, G.T., *A Personal Narrative of a Visit to Ghazni, Kabul and Afghanistan* (1840)

Williams, D.Elwyn, 'The Makers of the Sikh Army (1820–1850)', *The Army Quarterly* LVI (1948)

Engraving of the battle of Gujerat, 21 February 1849. Note the use of sword and shield by the Sikh regular infantry. Being inexpert in the use of their bayonets (M'Gregor said that 'the Sikh bayonet is nearly harmless in their hands'), they much preferred these traditional weapons for close combat, and would cast aside their discharged muskets and rush sword in hand against the enemy.

THE PLATES

A1: *Jagirdari* horseman, 1799–1849

Traditional Sikh cavalry tactics involved skirmishing from horseback with firearms. To achieve this successfully required good matchlocks and good horses, and the Sikhs are credited with both. Their matchlocks were well designed and relatively accurate, though they were rarely effective beyond 80–100 paces. Most had a decorated steel barrel and a straight butt inlaid with ivory, silver, brass, and damascened steel plates. Other cavalry arms typically comprised shield, pistols, lance, sword, and occasionally a bow. Representing as they did the kingdom's landed gentry, *Jagirdari* troops were usually colourfully attired and often splendidly equipped.

A2: Irregular infantryman, c.1815

Traditional Sikh dress consisted of turban, coat, shorts, scarf or cummerbund, and sometimes slippers. Knotting their long hair on the crown gave rise to the tall, peaked style of turban worn here, which was characteristic of the period under review. The usual colours for commoners' clothes were dark blue and white; scarves and turbans might be patterned or red, but garments were otherwise generally plain. Typical infantry arms were matchlock, sword and shield, but as late as the 1840s some still carried spears.

A3: Early regular infantryman, c.1810–20

Based on paintings of the 1830s, this is a Muslim (some such pictures are specifically captioned as 'Najibs'), hence his non-Sikh appearance. Uniforms only began to be introduced c.1808, and some units still lacked them as late as 1820, when four battalions seen in Lahore had 'little or no

BELOW AND OPPOSITE

Much worn, faded, and heavily repaired, the two Sikh flags now hanging in Lichfield Cathedral appear to be the same as those shown on page 38. One is red with a yellow border, while the other (that captured at Ferozeshah) was once black with a red border. Note their enormous size (roughly 8½ft x 7½ft wide), long streamers, and the very short exposed part of the poles. The red flag has three narrow gold horizontal bands and still shows a pattern of gold flowers scattered over its surface, but neither flag any longer bears a central device. (Michael Perry)

uniformity in their dress'. Attached to his belt are a cartridge holder (rather than the more usual powder horn) and an ammunition pouch.

B1: *Fauj-i-ain* officer, 1830s

Only in the *Fauj-i-khas* was there any attempt at regulating officers' dress; otherwise each officer of the regular army dressed as he pleased, 'according to his esprit de corps, his personal vanity, and the length of his purse'. French, British, and native styles were to be seen side by side or mixed together in every unit. Coats were rarely embroidered or braided alike (the volume of lace was considered an indicator of rank), and epaulettes were of all shapes and sizes. Most officers, however, wore a black heron feather in the turban.

B2: General Jean-Francois Allard, c.1835

European officers also wore what they liked, despite the existence of an official uniform. This consisted of a red or green velvet cap with a gold band and tassel; a Kashmiri shawl in winter or a white cloth cloak in summer; a blue

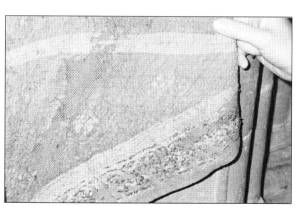

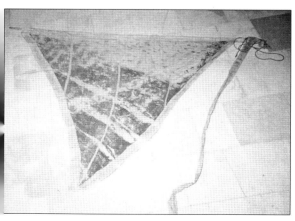

jacket 'not unlike that of [British] horse artillery'; a waistcoat, a shirt, and baggy scarlet trousers with a gold welt. Many were exotically attired: Gardner, for instance, wore a turban and a tartan suit, while Oms wore a Persian uniform of blue coat, gold epaulettes, white waistcoat, red trousers, and black lambskin cap. All Europeans in Sikh service were required to grow beards and moustaches.

B3: Maharaja Ranjit Singh, c.1835

By this date Ranjit Singh was small and frail, with a high forehead, raised eyebrows, a small upturned nose, and a greying beard and moustache. His cheeks were deeply scarred by an attack of smallpox suffered during childhood, which had also blinded him in his left eye. His dress was usually relatively plain by Sikh standards. His horse furniture was, by contrast, invariably opulent, saddlery and saddle cloths alike being decorated with emeralds, diamonds, turquoise, pearls, coral, silver and gold.

C1: *Fauj-i-ain* sepoy, 1820s

Uniforms had become commonplace by this time. European styles began to be adopted c.1810 and prevailed by the mid-1820s, but native types such as that worn here continued to be seen until the 1830s. Flintlocks – some of them bought from the EIC, others manufactured in Lahore – began to supplant matchlocks before 1812, and had largely replaced them throughout the *Fauj-i-ain* by 1827 (although several battalions armed with matchlocks were seen at Lahore as late as January 1836). Wrapping firearms up to protect them from dust on the march was common practice.

C2: *Fauj-i-ain* naik, 1830s–40s

In the 1830s and 1840s most Sikh uniforms followed the style of those worn by EIC sepoys. Typically they comprised a scarlet jacket with white braid stripes across the breast, blue trousers, and a turban. Regiments were distinguished by the colours of both facings and turbans (these were not necessarily the same), recorded colours for the latter being white, blue, red, yellow, pink, and green. The cut of the jacket is described as being of an 'old pattern', seemingly dating back to the Napoleonic era. Belts and equipment were most often of black leather. The fuller turban now often seen had probably originated with the kingdom's Muslim troops. Note that the Sikh army followed the British system of NCO rank chevrons.

C3: *Fauj-i-khas* sepoy, 1830s–40s

Fauj-i-khas battalions wore white rather than blue trousers, and their uniforms were of 'a neater and superior style' to those of other units. The different turban colours worn by the brigade's three nominally Sikh battalions were yellow, crimson, and pink. Percussion muskets had been introduced in 1825, and most of the regular army was equipped with them by the outbreak of the First Sikh War.

D1: *Fauj-i-ain* sepoy in winter dress, 1830s

Though their red jackets and blue trousers technically constituted *Fauj-i-ain* winter dress, troops operating in especially cold conditions – such as the army which invaded Ladakh in the Himalayas in 1834 – were issued with *poshteen* goatskin jackets. Gulab Singh of Jammu issued these to his own troops once every three years, and the same practice may have prevailed in the *Fauj-i-ain*. These were supplemented where possible by boots, and additional quilted and padded garments.

This painting commissioned by a British traveller is captioned in Persian *'Sawar i sher rajiman'*, and in English 'General Allard's Cavalry, Punjaub, 1838'. However, the *Rajman Sher Singh* alluded to in the Persian caption consisted of dragoons, whereas this is clearly a lancer. As explained in the commentary to Plate F2, he is probably a sowar of the 2nd Lancers. (By permission of the British Library. Or.1382)

D2: *Fauj-i-khas* Purbia sepoy, 1830s–40s

When Ranjit Singh introduced shakos c.1810, only his Purbia and Gurkha battalions would consent to wear them. The painting of c.1827–43, in a French collection, from which this figure comes is captioned 'Soldat Pourpié' (Hindustani Hindu soldier); but an almost identical, though uncoloured, figure in Honigberger's book is described as a 'Gorekhee Sepahee' (Gurkha sepoy). However, the *Fauj-i-khas*'s Gurkha battalion differed in wearing black shakos and dark green jackets with red facings. Note the tricolour-striped shako plume.

D3: *Fauj-i-ain* sepoy in summer dress, 1830s

In hot weather the entire *Fauj-i-ain* substituted white jackets and trousers, but retained their coloured turbans. It is probably indicative of the inefficiency of the Sikh commissariat department that these summer uniforms could also be seen in winter. In December 1827, for instance, Murray saw several battalions in white jackets and trousers; and in December 1838 Emily Eden saw a parade of red-turbaned infantry which she describes as resembling 'a white wall with a red coping'.

E1: *Aspi* artilleryman, 1825–46

Artillery uniforms had been introduced by c.1814, but the variety worn here – described by Barr as 'something like our own horse artillery' – was adopted in 1825. The trousers could be either white or blue-black like the jacket, while a white jacket could be substituted in hot weather. Although new uniforms were supposed to be issued every two years, Barr saw artillerymen 'badly dressed in old coats of divers colours'.

E2: *Jinsi* artilleryman, 1825–46

Sikh artillerymen carried long, straight swords of a variety called a *kirch*, with which they defended their guns to the death. The British considered Sikh artillerymen to be the bravest troops fielded against them: 'They were as good soldiers as ever took the field,' wrote one. 'They would not leave their guns; and when the bayonet was through them they threw their arms round the guns and kissed them, and died.'

E3: *Aspi* Muslim artilleryman, c.1840

Although Henry Martens' famous Sikh Wars prints invariably depict artillerymen in the distinctive busby-like turbans worn by the other two figures, the painting from which this figure is taken indicates that ordinary turbans were also worn, though perhaps only in Muslim units. In 1838 Barr saw *aspi* gunners wearing 'red turbans (the jemadars or officers' being of silk), which hang down so as to cover the back part of the neck'.

F1: *Fauj-i-ain* cuirassier, c.1839

When Allard returned from leave in France at the beginning of 1836 he brought with him 'a large consignment of arms', including 400 *carabinier* cuirasses (a handful of which still survive in Lahore). This inspired Ranjit Singh to raise two regiments of cuirassiers, the additional necessary armours being manufactured in Wazirabad. The cuirassiers' uniform is described by Barr in 1839 as 'a short blue coat and a pair of dark trousers with a narrow red stripe tightly strapped over Wellington boots and spurs'. Their arms appear to have comprised sword, carbine, and a pair of pistols, the pistols at least having been brought from France by Allard.

F2: Sowar, 2nd Lancers, 1838

It has to be supposed that this sowar, taken from a Sikh painting, belongs to the *Rajman Lansia Dugun*, since we know that the other Lancer regiment (the *Rajman Khas Lansia*) wore blue jackets with scarlet facings and 'a profusion of lace', and, being attached to the *Fauj-i-khas*, substituted French tricolour pennants at their lance heads, as well as, probably, white trousers. Both regiments were armed with a 12ft lance (one contemporary source specifically describes it as 'a Polish lance'), a light sabre, and pistols.

F3: Dragoon, c.1840

Sikh dragoons were trained to fight on foot and horseback, and carried a bayonet as well as a sword. Other arms comprised a carbine and two pistols. Saddlecloths were crimson with a blue-and-white striped border. Some units wore helmets in place of turbans. The different regiments were distinguished by their facings (buff, green, and yellow are all recorded) and perhaps by their turbans. At their surrender in March 1849, 'Avitabile's Dragoons [wore] red coats, with yellow facings, white turbans, and [white] trousers'.

G1: *Ghorchurra sardar*, 1799–1849

The *Ghorchurras* were proud, dashing, reckless, and skilled in the use of their lances and swords – but were utterly wanting in discipline, and virtually uncontrollable on the battlefield. Their readiness to engage in close combat meant that armour remained important despite the widespread adoption of firearms. However, only *sardars* could afford such complete armour as that shown here, most men making do with a mail corselet and a simple unadorned helmet. Sikh lances measured 10–15ft and were of steel, palm wood or bamboo, surmounted by a red or black tuft and a steel blade; those of affluent men might have lacquered or decoratively painted shafts.

G2: *Sardar*, c.1840

This is based on a portrait of artillery commander-in-chief Lehna Singh Majithia. Note that, although a general in the *Fauj-i-ain*, he wears the traditional attire of the Sikh upper class: a tunic, long baggy trousers, a close-fitting robe, and either a Kashmiri shawl wrapped around the waist and/or shoulders, or a loose-fitting gown called a *choga*.

G3: *Fauj-i-qilajat* infantryman, 1840s

The irregulars who constituted the greater part of the *Fauj-i-qilajat* were neither uniformed nor uniformly equipped, although it seems likely that all were provided with a firearm of some sort, most often a matchlock. Shields and swords were doubtless universal. The traditional Sikh shield was of buffalo hide or, less often, rhinoceros or crocodile hide. Usually it was lacquered black and had four gilt bosses, but some were red or brown.

A study by Emily Eden of *Akalis* armed with matchlocks, swords, pistols, and quoits. Note the differing dimensions of the last, which decreased in size to match the taper of the turban. Compare with Plate H. (ENI Library)

H1: *Ghorchurra Khas* sowar, 1838

Foreign visitors were invariably impressed by the glittering spectacle of Ranjit Singh's 'bodyguard' troops, described by Henry Havelock in 1838 as a 'disorderly though gorgeous rabble'. Although they might dress in 'all the colours of the rainbow', their clothes were most commonly of saffron yellow, red or green silk, and gold or silver brocade. Many were armoured like figure G1, while others wore padded garments capable of resisting a sword stroke or even the point of a lance. They were armed with *tulwar* swords, matchlocks, lances, pistols, and bows, and a shield was customarily slung on the back: eyewitnesses recorded how, when attacked by cavalry, Sikh horsemen 'met the British charge by lying flat on their horses' necks, with their heads protected by the thick turban and their backs by the shields'.

H2 & H3: *Akalis*, **1799–1849** The most distinctive feature of *Akali* dress was the tall dark blue or black *dastar bunga* turban, adorned with up to nine quoits plus knives and other small weapons. More quoits might be carried round the arms and neck. The rest of their dress generally comprised a blue tunic, a cummerbund, white shorts and slippers. They were always festooned with weapons: Henry Steinbach described them as having a sword in each hand, two more in the belt, a matchlock slung at the back, and four quoits round the turban. Masson writes that they were 'always armed in a most profuse manner. Some of them have half a dozen swords stuck about them and their horses, and as many pistols, and other arms.' Although often seen mounted, they seem invariably to have fought on foot.

INDEX

References to illustrations are shown in **bold**.
Plates are shown with page and caption locators in brackets.